TAKING HEART
AND MAKING SENSE

Taking Heart
and Making Sense

A NEW VIEW OF NATURE, FEELING AND THE BODY

KARIN LINDGAARD

A DISTANT MIRROR

First published in 2022 by A Distant Mirror

Copyright © 2022 Karin Lindgaard

ISBN 978-0-6488705-4-8

A DISTANT MIRROR

Web: adistantmirror.com
Email: admin@adistantmirror.com

KARIN LINDGAARD

Web: www.embodimentphilosophy.com
Email: karin@embodimentphilosophy.com

Contents

Introduction

TAKING HEART AND MAKING SENSE is something we must do many times in life. We all face challenges or reach junctures where we need to dig a little deeper, find a little optimism—to take heart—while we also settle on a way of understanding that seems useful and that we can live with—we make sense. But people do this in very different ways. Each person's perspective on their own life is different and it is often difficult to know how things really are for someone else, what their experience is like. Such separateness is a part of being human. That is a theme of this book and seems important to acknowledge early on; we are separate and individualised beings. But an even bigger theme of this book is that we are interconnected beings, with each other and with the natural world. The first point we already know, but the second needs explaining. Western culture currently does not seem to understand it. This book offers one way of explaining our interconnectedness along with our separateness. Feeling is central to both.

In our own lives, feeling is important to understand because it is always present, even if sometimes it is very quiet. It is not some part of our consciousness that we can add or take away. It is the foundational level of our experience—of the physical body but somehow more than the body because the present, feeling body is also formed of its history. Often this history will be outside our awareness, even as it continues in our functioning, in our reactions to situations and in our habits. Yet even when we are unaware, feeling interprets this history; it relates our present and past as we recognise situations, whether by a subtle sense or a tumultuous change.

In a broader social sense, the relevance and importance of understanding feeling cannot be overstated. Secular Western culture seems to be adrift, without a strong sense of the value of

1

life or the best way for human beings to live and engage with one another. One key reason for this lack of moorings is that human experience—and its relation to the broader nature—is not adequately accounted for by the narratives that underpin and influence Western culture. Feeling is rendered essentially meaningless by both science and postmodernism and genuine alternatives have yet to come to fruition, although they are certainly in the making. We need theory that can explain human feeling—and subjective, individual experience—while still affirming the importance of science and empirical research. Such theory should support rigorous knowledge and understanding of the world, while at the same time anchoring us in a stronger sense of meaning and value, of our individual and collective lives, and of our participation in the very process of life itself. It should help us to develop care and concern for others as well as to deal with the undeniable difficulties of life, the fear and insecurity inherent in being alive.

It is not easy to chart a path that explains the depth of our interconnectedness while acknowledging the uniqueness of individual experience. Yet, if we can do this, we can begin to understand how working with our own experience effects change beyond ourselves—reverberating through interactions, groups and societies. Accepting my feeling helps me to accept yours. Understanding my history helps me to understand yours. This occurs at a much deeper level than we currently appreciate. Even so, we must take care not to romanticise feeling. Experience can be painful and alienating, particularly if we don't understand how it arises. Our feelings can be confusing and contradictory, and can push us to act in ways we don't understand or later regret. Human beings are complex, perhaps unfathomably so. We are capable of inflicting immense suffering on one another. Yet we manage to live relatively peacefully together in many places, sustained and buoyed by mutual care and cooperation, despite our flaws and differences. Our capacity to care for and connect with each other exists deeply in the natural way of things.

Explaining human experience in a useful way requires that we move beyond the concept of the isolated individual that permeates so many aspects of contemporary life. People are largely understood as entirely separate from one another and from nature—unconstrained, self-reliant and in competition. When we see ourselves this way, we tend to instrumentalise the natural world as an entity entirely disconnected from us, which we can only exploit and attempt to control, rather than in which we participate. Indeed, many of the metaphors we use to describe life itself are based on a fantasy of control—brains control people, genes control cells, chemistry controls physiology, natural selection controls evolution. None of these are accurate. They are based in the underlying view that the world is made of physical things and that other outside forces move them.

This book puts forward a different view, that we need to understand the intricacy of interactions that form nature—including individual human beings—from the ground up. Here I am referring to metaphysics—our foundational concepts. Even if we think they are irrelevant, they are everywhere. In recent years, we have helplessly witnessed the unprecedented destruction of animal and plant life, some of it centuries old, in megafires on more than one continent. We have discovered an enormous garbage island floating in the Pacific Ocean and microscopic plastic particles in every level of the food chain. Even so, we continue to live in more or less the same way and to plunder ancient natural resources, all while having our lives turned upside down by the worldwide spread of a new disease. I cannot help but think that the view of the world as composed of lifeless matter creates death because this view does not engender the right kind of care and concern. But perhaps this is poetic license. What I am certain of is that ideas collectively shape us as much as actions, and that when we change our worldview we can observe new phenomena. One of the most important phenomena that comes into focus when we understand nature differently is that meaning is immanent in nature, in living processes. This helps us to both value life itself and to experience and reflect on our humanness. Meaning is immanent in the living body, in the natural world. We experience this first as feeling.

Human beings are in and of the natural world. We can develop perspectives on the world, but we cannot stand outside it and view it objectively. A different underlying worldview can help us to come to terms with this without leading us into the idea that truth is relative—and the nihilism this idea leads to. This book in no way disagrees with the value of science and empirical research. Rather, it provides a broader view that highly values scientific inquiry while acknowledging the limits of the ideal of impartial observation. Many of the theories discussed in this book, which form its overall argument, are interpretations of empirical research. The purpose of presenting an alternative metaphysics as part of this argument is to develop a foundation that is already strongly implied in some branches of science, particularly biology and cognitive science. We are possibly on the verge of a paradigm shift.

This book deals with complex ideas from a variety of disciplines. Interdisciplinary work involves a different set of constraints than specialised academic work. I have tried to provide enough detail that the key points of theories are covered but not so much detail as to overwhelm the reader. Academic disciplines have become more and more specialised in recent decades—at the same time as pressures on academics have increased manifold because universities are now run as businesses rather than institutions for the public good. The result is a proliferation of highly specialised publications that no one can keep abreast of along with the general decline of funding to the pure humanities and sciences—areas of research that do not directly generate financial revenue for institutions. In this way, and to our detriment, the entire system we live under replicates itself.

With the intention of resisting this fragmentation of knowledge, I have based most of this book on discussions of books that are already syntheses of research. They are all written by scholars and scientists. Some are meant for a more general readership while some are more specialised, but they all offer thorough arguments and many draw on empirical research. This means that interested readers can easily follow up discussions. It also means that I can treat these books as texts in themselves. I assume that all the research they report is sound, so I can work with the specific ideas and themes they each put forward as well as make connections between them to further my own argument. This is the way I have learnt to do interdisciplinary research and it is not perfect because it cannot properly acknowledge all the scholars dedicated to specialised research. It also cannot fully explain the intricacies of theories and debates within particular fields. Still, I believe it is a valid endeavour and can help to overcome fragmentation while demonstrating an important role for philosophy in this endeavour, and in public life much more generally.

One of the areas in which scientific understanding has progressed rapidly in the past two decades is the field of neuroscience. Recent themes that are relevant to theories of feeling are the brain's role in homeostasis (life regulation) and interoception (sensing or representing the inner state of the body). These themes are obviously related to each other and are important for how we understand the arising of experience—or feeling. While much has been discovered about these key processes, extrapolations about whole body functioning, behaviour and experience are often either partly or completely described through those metaphors of separation and control, with the brain as an ultimate regulator. This can lead to far-reaching conclusions about human life that I see as unhelpful and inaccurate, conclusions which cannot help us to consider how best to live or how best to deal with collective problems beyond optimising our own separate experience. They do not help us to understand meaning and value in and with the world.

Questions about life functioning, inner sensing and experience should instead be seen in terms of the whole body as a particular kind of system in particular kinds of relationships. Thus, rather than asking how the brain controls the body or how the brain constructs meaning, we need to ask how whole systems regulate themselves and how whole systems look at themselves. Then, even more importantly, we need to consider how systems understand themselves in relation to other systems and other phenomena. These questions uncover the need to reconsider our most basic assumptions about reality and reconstruct a worldview based on different assumptions. While such a project is in some respects very abstract and is conceptually demanding, a new perspective gradually emerges that encourages and makes space for a much deeper appreciation of the intricacy, the inherent value, the symphonic interwovenness of the natural world and the profoundly creative process of evolution. This beautiful, shimmering, changing wholeness includes our humanness in relation—our tender vulnerability and our unique potential. These are big, ambitious themes but we need such themes to help carry us through to a genuinely new way of being with each other and within the natural world. My hope is that this book will become part of the chorus that can do this.

Rather than simply announcing the need for a new metaphysics, Part One of this book demonstrates this need by discussing some key theories of emotion and feeling in psychology, cognitive science, philosophy and neuroscience. The intention here is twofold—to offer concepts and details that are important and useful for a theory of feeling as well as to highlight limitations in each perspective that point to the need for change at a more fundamental level. Chapters one to three therefore provide background theory as well as setting the scene for the theory that follows. Most works referred to in detail are recent publications but trajectories of development, particularly within cognitive science, over the past twenty-five years are also referenced.

Part Two—chapters four to seven—offers a theory of nature based on a new set of fundamental assumptions. I first clarify why this is necessary—in chapter four—by discussing the dualistic thinking that underlies the history of Western thought and continues to pervade Western culture. Chapter five outlines and justifies new categories to base our worldview on. I suggest that *change* is the fundamental characteristic that we can identify in any phenomenon and discuss a way of building *perspective* into the way we think about things. We may not have absolute knowledge of anything but we can develop stable and meaningful perspectives. We can do this by understanding the world as formed of processes, always existing in relation to other processes. The basic orientation here—of process/relation—is inside/outside. Current ideas in theoretical biology are explained in chapters six and seven so that we can better understand how living systems function both within themselves and in relation to other systems and phenomena. Understanding life in this way means that we can more easily see creativity and interconnectedness as fundamental to the natural world. Meaning is immanent in nature, including in human life.

The best way to bring such theories of nature into a new way of understanding feeling is by first understanding behaviour. This helps to keep our theorising stable, in the manner of science, because we observe living systems from the outside. This is especially important for observing animals. We can see what they do without assuming anything about how they feel. Part three—chapters eight to ten—makes the transition from understanding behaviour to suggesting a different way of looking at feeling. In chapter eight I develop an idea of behaviour as complex attunements to create harmony amongst levels inside and outside of a system; and chapter nine further supports this by discussing the neuroscience of implicit learning and memory. Finally, in chapter ten, I can speak about feeling as a holistic, inner sensing—a *sense of fit*. This concept is a way of understanding how animals move through their lives with feeling. They recognise situations and on some level recognise themselves, even if they may not experience the same emotions as human beings. As the *sense of fit* helps us to understand animal lives as meaningful for them, it also allows us to be clearer about just how much of our human behaviour is habitual and automatic, and in that sense nonconscious.

Part Four then deals with human experience. Chapter eleven looks at human behaviour from the perspective of interactions among people and in groups before chapter twelve connects this perspective to a theory of infant development. Finally, in chapter thirteen, I describe a new way of understanding feeling—as *unique, individual metaphors*. This explains how our human feeling is built up in our histories but also emerges creatively in present-time situations. It means that our personal experience is stable and meaningful, created in concert with others, but that it is not fixed or essential; it can change. Chapter fourteen explores how feeling and language interact in the ongoing gestalt of conscious experience. Language is more precise but feeling is more honest. Neither should be prioritised—they are simply different forms of understanding that function in relation to one another. I suggest that attending to feeling along with thoughtful, even rational deliberation brings out the creative potential of consciousness as a process. We can become more present with ourselves and with each other.

In conclusion, I mention some of the ramifications of the overall view of feeling developed, particularly in relation to the underlying speculative metaphysics. While tentative, they can lead to a very different perspective on our human relations. We are quite literally in this together. Thus, even though this book does not directly deal with the current global environmental issues, I believe that a better understanding of human feeling—along with the fundamental nature of the evolutionary processes through which human experience has arisen—could offer a much needed, but complementary counterpart to the increasingly desperate voices of so many esteemed scientists. We must not only change the way we live *materially* but we must care for and cooperate with one another to do so. We must value life in a new way.

PART 1

CONTEMPORARY PERSPECTIVES

1

From emotion concepts to embodied cognition

Feeling and emotion

How can we distinguish between feeling and emotion—and indeed, should we? We often refer to our emotions as feelings, and at times we might identify that we feel emotional. Even so, the two are certainly not the same. When I say that "I *am* sad" I convey something subtly, but significantly different than if I say "I *feel* sad". The first could be a bigger statement, perhaps about how I generally am or how I see myself in relation to a particular state of affairs in my life, but the second usually refers more clearly to my present, bodily state. I might even identify a present feeling of sadness without knowing why I currently have it. At the same time, if we are talking about feeling states, emotions seem more specific. Feeling can cover all sorts of experiences: hungry, restless, warm, alert. Understanding these differences is important for discussing how we inhabit, identify, and refer to our experience. While we tend to use the terms emotion and feeling somewhat interchangeably in everyday life, a theory of feeling should make a clear distinction. Such a theory must also explain and find a place for emotion.

One reason for beginning this book with theories about emotion is that they seem to be more common than theories about feeling. Emotion has figured more strongly in the history of philosophy—notably because of its identification with the passions, and thereby its difference from reason or rationality. Many philosophers from the Ancient Greeks onwards have seen emotion and the passions as central to the consideration of ethics—although not always in opposition to reason; the Stoics initiated a tradition that views emotions as evaluative judgments and therefore kinds of cognition.[1] Even so, the theme of emotions as distinct from reason has been strongly present in psychology, with emotion seen as separate from—even in opposition to—cognition. However, developments in cognitive science, psychology and neuroscience, over the past twenty years, have been breaking down this distinction.[2] Emotion has also received much more attention in philosophy recently, even in the Anglo-American tradition, which has traditionally been disparaging of emotion.[3] Such work is necessary and important but the relationship between emotion and feeling is often unclear, if feeling is mentioned at all.

When scientists, and some philosophers, do mention feeling they often refer to it as *affect*. Affect describes the ever-present and bodily aspect of feeling, in terms of two parameters. One parameter—*valence*—refers to the pleasantness or unpleasantness of bodily sensations, while the other—*arousal*—describes the degree of calmness or agitation you feel.[4] Some researchers attempt to disentangle a third parameter that relates to control, such as *potency* or *dominance*.[5] Affect often seems to be treated quite distinctly from emotion without clarifying the relation between the two—although a default relation might be that emotion is a broader event with affect the subjective phase or experience of that event.[6] But *feeling* seems to me to be much more than affect. Feeling seems more holistic and meaningful than these two (or perhaps, three) parameters, even though feeling must *also* include the every-present bodily aspect of affect. These points are not just splitting hairs. They relate to the complexity of our experience, to how we think and talk about experience and how this in turn further influences our experience. Thus, while I ultimately intend to create a theory about feeling, I will start by examining a theory of emotion.

Emotion is ambiguous because at times it refers to strong

behavioural responses, at other times to strong feeling experiences, or even sometimes to both. One reason for this is that—according to our everyday understanding of emotion—we often behave emotionally without paying attention to the feeling of the emotion. This is particularly true for very strong emotions. When they overtake us we feel more *in* them, more *doing* them than experiencing them. We have all witnessed others behaving emotionally who seem unaware of it: "I'm not angry!!"—erupting from a tense face, eyes blazing— "*You're* just being…" That we might display emotions without feeling them, or while feeling something else that we are not necessarily identifying with emotion comes through in the historical background of the terms themselves.

The word *emotion* originates in part from the Latin ēmōtiōn—em, meaning "of action", or ē-movrē, from (ē) "out" and (move-re) "to move"—therefore meaning "to move out". The earlier uses were literally about moving or migrating from one place to another, physical stirrings or agitation, or social and political disturbance. A relation between agitation and conscious experience followed: emotion could refer to "Any disturbance of mind, feeling, passion." Later, emotion came to refer to a distinct *kind* of conscious experience separate from other forms of cognition and intention.[7]

The term *feeling*, on the other hand, developed from associations with inner experience and the sense of touch. It appears to have been associated literally with the sense of touch that relies on physical contact: "To examine or explore by touch", but also more generally with conscious experience; feeling the inner or mental effects of something. Feeling is an older term, present in Old English, whereas emotion is dated to the mid-1500s.[8]

While feeling and emotion have become somewhat mutually defining—with one definition of feeling being "the condition of being emotionally affected"—we should keep the separate origins of the terms in mind. Emotion is historically related to action and agitation, and feeling to sensing and understanding. The *moving out* aspect of emotion denotes that either we are trying to effect some kind of change in the world around us or that we release an inner pressure in some other way—crying when sad for instance. This is not to say that people do not *feel* emotions—of course people often feel sad when they cry, although they may feel many other things—but rather that emotions are not clearly definable as either conscious or unconscious. Feeling on the other hand must be conscious; it is an awareness. These differences and why they matter will be explained with more detail and clarity through this book. For the moment the distinction is worth keeping in mind as we reflect on existing theories, and whether they emphasise one or the other of these definitions.

A new theory of emotion: Barrett's emotion concepts

Many readers will be familiar with the classical view of emotions put forward in psychology. Proponents of this view understand emotions as *essences*—the idea that common emotions exist objectively in human beings, identifiable by their distinct and traceable patterns in the brain, body and experience. These emotions are considered as having developed through evolution. They are therefore *wired in* and present from birth. While emotion has long been associated with animal behaviour and expression, the modern view of innate emotional responses began in the late nineteenth century, with Charles Darwin's *The Expression of the Emotions in Man and Animals*, and was further developed by William James, whose work on emotion remains widely cited in psychology. From the mid-twentieth century onwards, psychologists established a theory of basic emotions, building on Silvan Tomkins' concept that innate responses of emotion were driven by *affect programs* in the brain.[9] No consensus currently exists as to which emotions are basic; contemporary psychologists put forward varying lists. However, well-known emotion theorist, Paul Ekman, and Daniel Cordaro state unambiguously: "There is evidence for universality in the following seven emotions": anger, fear, surprise, sadness, disgust, contempt and happiness.[10] Basic emotions are understood as automatically generated. They can happen quickly and be very brief. They are distinguished from other so-called affective states, such as mood—which do not possess universal distinguishing features—and from blended emotions and more complex adaptations developed through experience.

Despite its prominence, this theory has been strongly refuted. Many researchers in psychology have tried to find the patterns or *fingerprints* for these basic emotions. However, as Lisa Feldman Barrett reports in her book *How Emotions Are Made: The Secret Life of the Brain*, research over the past twenty years has failed to find strong evidence for the classical view. Barrett and her research team have carried out numerous studies as well as summarising extensive prior research in meta-reviews. Some more recent studies make use of brain imaging; for instance studies can involve inducing emotions in test participants with images, scenarios or cognitive tasks while data about brain functioning is collected. Rather than finding distinct patterns of activity and expression, they find a great deal of variation; for example a subjective experience labelled as fear might result from very different underlying physiological changes, brain patterns and facial expressions. Equally, the same patterns that produce an experience of fear might also produce a different experience—say, surprise—in a different context.

While Barrett's research finds no clear evidence for emotion fingerprints, it does report other important findings, particularly about the patterns of brain functioning that appear to underlie emotion. One of the most interesting of these findings is how much emotion appears to be related to both interoception and homeostasis—sensing and regulating the internal state of the body. These two aspects of brain and body functioning are currently attracting much attention in the study of emotion and feeling. Barrett explains interoception as the brain's *representation* of sensations from the body. These sensations are the result of the inner movements and physiological changes occurring all the time in the body. Interoception is the source of experiences of both emotion and feeling:

> Usually, you experience interoception only in
> general terms: those simple feelings of pleasure,
> displeasure, arousal, or calmness... Sometimes,
> however, you experience moments of intense
> interoceptive sensations as emotions.[11]

She says that interoception is a whole brain process, but also details the way that several brain regions work together as an *interoceptive network* within this whole process. This network involves areas that represent sensations from the body (primary interoceptive cortex) as well as areas that survey the energy needs of the body (body-budgeting regions). The notion of body-budgeting is explained in terms of the brain's need to anticipate the energy needs of the body. For example, when the brain perceives the need for a burst of energy, the body-budgeting regions instruct the adrenal gland to release cortisol, which then floods the bloodstream with glucose, making energy available for cells.

The key point here is *anticipation*—the idea of energy needs that may be *about to* occur in relation to people or situations. Anticipation, in turn, needs to be understood in relation to simulation. Simulation, as used by Barrett, seems to refer to two kinds of activity, both arguably on the border of conscious awareness. It refers to the fact that activity in the brain—for example thoughts about particular actions or body movements or even watching images of others moving—results in actual changes in the body, which results in interoceptive sensations, or feelings.

> We now have good evidence that your brain
> predicts your body's responses by drawing on prior
> experience with similar situations and objects, even
> when you're not physically active.[12]

This is understood as simply an aspect of *intrinsic brain activity*—the fact that the brain is constantly active, maintaining the internal functioning of the body but also continuously assessing and anticipating, including when we are not actively engaged.

Intrinsic brain activity is also the source of "dreams, daydreams, imagination, mind wandering and reveries".[13] Barrett reports that:

> As it turns out, people spend at least half their
> waking hours simulating rather than paying
> attention to the world around them, and this pure
> simulation strongly drives their feelings.[14]

These concepts lead to one of the central ideas offered by Barrett: prediction. The key theme is that the brain predicts what the energy needs of the body *will be* in a given situation and that prediction results in physiological and interoceptive changes, as the brain essentially tells the body what to do. Feelings and emotions are the result:

> Every brain region that's claimed to be a home of
> emotion in humans is a body-budgeting region
> within the interoceptive network. These regions,
> however, don't react in emotion. They don't react
> at all. They predict, intrinsically, to regulate your
> body budget.[15]

Thus, feeling and emotion, as emerging from interoception, are essentially explained as the result of predictions. As predictions they can only be based on past experience. While Barrett does mention feeling, she focuses much more on emotion. This is partly because her point of departure is to refute the classical view, with its naming of basic and generic emotions and its dynamic of rather mechanistically triggered emotion patterns. The interesting result of bringing together her position with the multitude of studies and evidence she presents—evidence which, as said, proposes that emotions are not reactions but predictions—is that emotions are recast as concepts. Once she has explained prediction in terms of simulation and interoception, she then presents this epiphany—that emotions are actually *concepts*. They become something we learn. Without the concept, or word, for a particular emotion, we simply do not experience it. Emotions are labels that we attach to certain patterns of sensation in particular situations. No label, no emotion.

Importantly, Barrett is not saying that emotions do not exist or that in the absence of concepts we do not experience anything; this is why feeling gets a mention. We might have feeling, explained as affect, yet no distinct emotion as such. Thus we have feeling in the ever-present and of-the-body sense mentioned earlier. Indeed, Barrett uses this claim to say that animals may have affect but not emotion. Emotions are a social reality. They are terms we agree upon that enable us to understand and speak about various experiences across situations. Emotions become a mental phenomenon, like other concepts. Feeling, or affect is essentially meaningless, seen as a kind of by-product of interoception, the purpose of which is to provide information for the brain to regulate the body-budget.

Confused? Me too. Barrett's research is meticulous and her ideas compelling but the dynamics of the processes she names—interoception, simulation, prediction—are difficult to grasp. Her theory also reaches some strange conclusions. Barrett makes big claims for prediction. She says, "Everything you feel is based on prediction from your knowledge and past experience."[16] Not *some* or even *most* of what you feel, but *all* of it. However, she reports, "While predictive brain circuitry is important for affect, it is likely not necessary."[17] This suggests that interoception from the body, in the moment, generating affect is possible. She might mean here that we can experience *meaningless sensations* from the body, but these are not really feelings—presumably they are affect without valence. Feelings and emotions rely on prediction and are conceptual in their nature.

These ideas are outlined in relation to homeostasis, the ongoing regulation that maintains bodily processes within appropriate ranges for survival. Linking the continuous activity of the brain and body that keeps us alive to feeling and emotion opens up important areas for discussion. It highlights that our perceptions of and responses to what is going on around us are always in relation to maintaining life and stability. In our everyday understanding, feelings and emotions seem to come and go, but Barrett's work emphasises the continuous homeostatic background against which this takes place. This is evident in the body budget concept as well as the explanation of intrinsic brain activity, which is just that constant change and monitoring.

Unfortunately, though, her approach—which is a feature of traditional neuroscience more generally—characterises the brain as an *ultimate regulator*. For Barrett the ongoing regulation of bodily processes, anticipated by the brain, results in all our interoceptive sensations: "intrinsic brain activity... ultimately produces every sensation you experience, including your interoceptive sensations".[18] So by anticipating the needs of the body, the brain directs changes in the body while also representing sensations. These sensations may be organised by emotion concepts for full-blown emotional experiences. All of this is directed in and by the brain, which becomes the centre of agency: "And so, trapped within the skull, with only past experiences as a guide, your brain makes *predictions*".[19] This means that the brain is "wired for delusion".[20] It leads to the stunning claim that "you are an architect of your experience"[21] although given that we have no awareness of the predictive processes—in that we believe we are perceiving and responding to what is actually happening—the notion of *you* becomes fairly meaningless.

An important feature of Barrett's work is that it describes top-down causation. The classical view of emotion does the opposite; it is an example of bottom-up causation. In this view an experience of emotion is caused by various underlying physiological and neurological changes as reactions to various sensory perceptions coming directly from outside. A top-down understanding of emotions as concepts means that they have organising power over experience. The concept itself activates physiological changes, either fed back or represented as interoceptive sensation. However, this top-down model still seems to describe a linear causal sequence, whereas top-down causation suggests more complex causal interactions. Granted, we do often think about causes as operating in a linear fashion. Our everyday thinking about causation tends to be mechanistic and reliant on one-to-one relations. But our habit of linear thinking can become confusing and contradictory—particularly when positioning the brain as ultimate regulator. The role of the body and particularly the relation of interoception to an *actual* body becomes very unclear. The suggestion that we are architects of our own experience also downplays the role of the *actual* circumstances in which we find ourselves to the point of almost disregarding them.

Barrett does leave room for adjusting to actual situations, described as resolving prediction error. She also refers to the similar process of tinkering—which is the role of a so-called *control network* in the brain—and which Barrett explains should best be seen as an optimizer rather than a controller. She describes a process of weighting the importance of different types of incoming information to "regulate your body budget, produce a stable perception, and launch an action".[22] This may be the most interesting and important aspect of the whole process because it describes a responding, in the moment, to that which actually occurs. Understanding this process might temper the excesses of choice implied in her more sweeping statements. Importantly, "much of this tinkering happens outside your awareness".[23] How might this tinkering be in our awareness, or brought to awareness? If we act and feel so much as a result of our past experiences how *do* we relate to our bodies and our worlds in the present? We may not be open to the world—perceptually and emotionally—in the way we usually believe, but how *do* we engage with the world even if we do not have an objective view of it? Barrett's research introduces important concepts, but these become obscured in the overall view of us as isolated, closed systems. This seems ironic in the setting of social constructionism, although matches it in its belief that all knowledge and experience is ultimately relative or subjective.

Towards a more embodied view

Given that Barrett describes emotions as concepts, yet the relation to the body is unclear, it makes sense to consider her ideas in relation to the field of embodied cognition. This interdisciplinary field has been growing for the past few decades and particularly since the beginning of the twenty-first century. In fact, embodiment has become something of a buzzword in many areas of scholarship; it is not an exaggeration to say that it is one of the major developing themes across the humanities. Being interdisciplinary, embodied cognition is still a disparate field with many viewpoints; one summary describes it as "a loose-knit family of research programs in the cognitive sciences".[24] In his book *Enactivist Interventions*, Shaun Gallagher elaborates, "in some respects it is more like a philosophical framework for research in those sciences".[25] Gallagher provides an insightful overview of various theories of embodied cognition and explains their relation to aspects of traditional cognitive science. He offers a more nuanced approach than the way embodied cognition is often presented, as in opposition to traditional cognitive science, the theoretical perspective that preceded it. Different views within embodied cognition are not inherently and equally opposed to traditional views, but instead encompass a variety of responses to issues in cognitive science.

Traditional cognitive science rose to prominence in the 1950s and 60s. It was based on a computational theory of cognition and was highly influenced by developments in computing and Artificial Intelligence. The scientific and technical achievements of these times held great hope for understanding cognition as essentially rational computation in the mind. The computer was the metaphor *par excellence* for understanding the mind. If the process of cognition was essentially computation—the logical and abstract manipulation of symbols—then symbols must exist somehow, abstractly, in the mind. Thus, the computational theory goes hand in hand with representationalism, the idea that the mind conceptually *represents* external reality so that it may then reason about the world, make decisions and so on.

Researchers in embodied cognition present an array of critiques of and responses to this view, but they all share an understanding of the body as having an important role in cognition:

> Embodiment thesis: Many features of cognition are
> embodied in that they are deeply dependent upon
> characteristics of the physical body of an agent, such that
> the agent's beyond-the-brain body plays a significant causal
> role, or a physically constitutive role, in that agent's
> cognitive processing.[26]

24

Some developments in embodied cognition have focused on how processes we would usually consider more basic level *perceptions* are involved in the generation of more abstract *concepts*. One area that has received sustained attention is the role of sensory and motor areas of the brain in cognition, investigated with neuroimaging while people perform various cognitive tasks. Researchers have collected much empirical evidence in support of the participation of sensory and motor systems in *higher order* thinking.[27] In simpler terms, this evidence implies that understanding words or objects associated with activity employs areas of the brain that direct actual body movement in that person. Brain areas that govern physical activity are activated in situations in which the person is not actually moving or preparing for movement. A mounting body of neuroscientific evidence exists to support this, but various interpretations are possible. Different interpretations essentially ascribe different causal roles for—and thereby different levels of importance to—the body in processes of cognition. The understanding and role of *representation* can differ significantly among different interpretations, as can the overall sense of the relation between brain and body, and indeed brain, body and world.

That sensory and motor systems within the brain are activated during, for example, language processing, challenges the view in traditional cognitive science that abstract concepts—which are seen as the basis of reasoning—exist separately in the brain and mind. This includes challenging the notion of a truly compartmentalised brain. However, accepting this empirical evidence does not necessarily go against more traditional views of computation and representation. We can see this in Barrett's theory, especially with regard to simulation. Simulation is difficult to understand because we can imagine it as more or less involved with what is actually going on in the body—the brain may be doing this more or less independently of the body. Indeed, some researchers in embodied cognition have made a distinction between *shallow* and *deep* processing. How much the sensory or motor systems—of both brain and body—are involved might be related to the degree of ambiguity in a situation.[28]

As already mentioned in the discussion of Barrett's work, interoception and homeostasis are receiving more attention as important, perhaps central, to thinking and acting in all areas of everyday life and decision making. Simulation, in this case, relates to interior bodily states and in Barrett's formulation is essentially representation. The brain uses these representations—which appear to be numerous in any given instance—to then form an inference or *best guess* about the upcoming needs of the body. This is a predictive processing model, which is entirely consistent with computation. The brain receives information and makes inferences by way of complex computational processes. Actual physiological changes seem to be another version of *sense data* or information from the environment that the brain receives and then directs. While there must be causal feedback because the brain both receives and generates physiological information, the brain is portrayed as an isolated agent, obscuring any significant causal role for the body. Thus, while the body *appears* to be important, it is essentially an *instrument* of the brain. Gallagher makes the same point in relation to predictive coding models of cognition and considers this position a weak form of embodiment—so weak in fact that versions of embodied cognition with a much stronger causal role for the body may not even recognise it as embodied cognition.

It is worth reflecting on the broader background from which Barrett's research emerges—the psychology of emotion—as opposed to that of embodied cognition, which emerged (at least partly) in the philosophy of mind and cognition. Barrett responds to the classical view of emotion in psychology, which sees emotion as body-based. It describes emotion as stable patterns of change in physiology and expression. Because her research finds no fixed patterns of response in or with the body, and frames emotion as the brain's concept of what needs to happen in the body, emotion becomes more of a phenomenon of the mind. Conversely, embodied cognition finds that what have for a long time been understood as phenomena of the mind are actually deeply engaged with the body—the question is then how deeply. However, embodied cognition has not been centrally concerned with emotion and feeling, because it began with theories about language and abstract thinking. So in a very real sense, these two areas have had opposite trajectories, even though both are breaking down the distinction between mind and body in important ways. It is for this reason that aspects of the way Barrett presents emotion should be preserved, but within a different philosophical framework. Some of the insights generated in embodied cognition research can support an understanding of emotion as similar to what we normally term *concepts* but also deeply emergent from the body and strongly connected to an environment as well as a person's history—away from the *isolated brain in the skull* perspective. A closer look at and better understanding of feeling, as distinct from emotion, is of central importance to this project.

Specific theories

Two streams of embodied cognition are relevant for a theory of feeling as strongly embodied and environmentally situated—as well as aligned with the view of emotions as concepts. The first stream bases its understanding of cognition on a theory of metaphor. Metaphor is seen as the process by which phenomena that are more easily understood in everyday life are projected onto other, less clear phenomena so that we can define and speak about them. The classic early work in this field, George Lakoff and Mark Johnson's *Metaphors We Live By* was published in 1987. This book was a major inspiration for the field of embodied cognition and much research followed, with metaphor as a basis for philosophy detailed in *Philosophy in the Flesh* by the same authors. Later work by Mark Johnson—in particular *The Meaning of the Body*, published in 2007—is also an important influence on the theory being developed here.

The second stream of embodied cognition important to this project is enactivism. Influenced by phenomenological philosophy, biology and Buddhist views of mind, its beginnings are often traced to Francisco Varela, Evan Thompson and Eleanor Rosch's *The Embodied Mind*, published in 1991. The enactivist tradition also includes philosophers such as Alva Noë—whose book *Out of Our Heads* is an accessible introduction to an enactivist perspective—and Sean Gallagher whose book *Enactivist Interventions* has already been mentioned. Enactivism conceptualises cognition as an ongoing dynamic interaction with an environment. It proposes a strong version of embodiment that focuses on our continuous present-time engagement with situations, often described as *structural coupling* to an environment. One area in which enactivism has had much influence is in the understanding of perception—in particular visual perception—as an active process made possible by a living body in dynamic engagement with its surroundings.

Both streams of embodied cognition and their particular relevance for a theory of feeling will be discussed in the following two chapters, to show how they complement one another and how they suggest the need for a different underlying metaphysical framework. At this stage it is worth noting that they both have been characterised as approaches that take the body as a *constraint* on cognition, meaning that we understand the world in certain ways by virtue of the kinds of bodies we have.[29] For the metaphor stream this means that those phenomena that form the basis for metaphors are related to the kinds of bodies we have and the kinds of experiences and interactions that are the natural result of being in our human bodies. For the enactivist stream the body as a constraint on cognition comes through as a more direct relationship—in the style of phenomenology—of a dynamic, living body in interaction:

> cognition is a dynamic sensorimotor activity, and
> the world that is given and experienced is not only
> conditioned by the neural activity of the subject,
> but is essentially enacted in that it emerges through
> the bodily activities of the organism.[30]

These different approaches to the ways the body constrains cognition can be understood in relation to the idea of representation. The metaphor stream can be interpreted as compatible with traditional notions of representation while the enactivist stream is not. Lakoff and Johnson at times explain the workings of metaphor with reference to neural structures—suggesting metaphorical projection from one domain of experience to another may take place entirely within the brain. Thus, sensory and motor experiences may form kinds of understanding, which exist as neural structures that form the basis for understanding via metaphor in other domains, such as abstract concepts. Seen in this way, the metaphor stream constitutes a weak form of embodiment. If we simply extend bodily activity to include interoception, then this view is consistent with Barrett's view—also a weak form of embodiment. However, Lakoff and Johnson do not see their work as subscribing to representation as involving existent structures within the brain. They explain, "the only workable theory of representations is one in which a representation is a flexible pattern of organism-environment interactions, and not some inner mental entity that somehow gets hooked up with parts of the external world".[31] The idea of flexible patterns of interaction provides an important link to the enactivist conception of cognition, and can also relate somewhat to

Barrett's work—to her insistence that the process of inference is dynamic. To better comprehend these links, we first need a deeper understanding of the theories of metaphor and enactivism. As a preliminary suggestion, to be further explained in the following two chapters, we can say that metaphor tends to focus more on *structure*, while enactivism focuses more on *dynamic engagement*. Not only are both relevant, but the relation between them is a key conceptual thread of this book.

2

The co-creation of experience and understanding

Metaphor

IT IS TEMPTING TO THINK of metaphor as simply a function of language—a way that language elaborates from descriptions of experience that are somehow simpler or more direct to realms that are more nebulous or, some would say, poetic. This keeps metaphor in line with objectivist theories of truth and language, which are compatible with traditional views of cognition. However Lakoff and Johnson's theory takes a very different view of metaphor. When they say that "the human conceptual system is metaphorically structured and defined",[1] they mean that metaphor profoundly shapes not only our understanding but also our experience in ways that we are not usually aware of.

> *The essence of metaphor is understanding and experiencing one kind of thing in terms of another.*[2]

To offer an introductory example, we commonly use our understanding of journeys to define and speak about relationships. We might *set out* with someone, which might be an entirely *new path* for us. Things could *go along smoothly* for a while but then after an *obstacle* we become unsure *where the relationship is going*. We might decide to end it or *continue on the journey*, which could go *in various directions*. While all of these expressions might seem obvious in the way they refer to relationships, they involve the metaphorical projection of one kind of experience (a journey) onto another (a relationship). The concept of travelling along a path helps us to organise our experience and understanding of being in a relationship.

Given that we can organise some of our understanding and experience by way of other experiences, via metaphorical projection, we might then easily assume that some of our experiences are more *basic* or *direct* than others—such as journeys, which can metaphorically organise our understanding and experience of relationships. However, this is not the case; Lakoff and Johnson carefully avoid the idea that some experiences are more basic than others. While much of their early work with metaphor is well explained, with many accessible examples and discussions of linguistic metaphors, some of it remains obscure. This is partly because their theory relies on discussions of language, a problem that they acknowledge themselves; in *Metaphors We Live By*, they admit that "We do not know very much about the experiential bases of metaphor".[3]

What Lakoff and Johnson do say, however, is that some experiences—namely, physical experiences—are more *clearly delineated* than others. They explain:

> We typically conceptualize the nonphysical *in terms* of the physical – that is, we conceptualize the less clearly delineated in terms of the more clearly delineated.[4]

Importantly, those experiences that are more clearly delineated are not more basic. For instance, Lakoff and Johnson use the term *natural kinds* of experience to describe experiences that may be *either more or less* clearly delineated. Examples of natural kinds of experience that are more clearly delineated, and therefore used to metaphorically define other experiences, are physical orientations, objects, substances, seeing, journeys and war. Examples of natural kinds of experience that are less clear and may be defined by these (or other clear experiences) are love, time, ideas, understanding, happiness and health.

To illustrate, the metaphors *happy is up* and *sad is down* (an example that is often cited) follow this pattern. Physical orientation (up and down) is projected onto emotion (happy and sad) and then informs many metaphors that we use to speak about being happy or sad. We might say "She was on a high after acing the test", or "He's over the moon about the new job". Or "She's been really down since they broke up" or "I'm in a low mood today". These metaphors, extrapolated from the basic orientation *happy is up, sad is down* are based in genuine correlations in our bodily experience; happiness tends to be associated with a more upright posture and sadness with a more slumped posture. That this metaphor holds culturally doesn't rely on these associations being fixed; happiness doesn't always coincide with upright posture, and upright posture on its own certainly doesn't define happiness, but the correlation happens enough for the metaphor to be understood. Then, for an experience that is less clear, such as an emotion, we can use all manner of expressions for different intensities or qualities of a given emotion—being *over the moon* expresses more than saying *very happy*, while being *down in the dumps* has a different quality than *a bit low*, and both say more than *very sad* or *a bit sad*.

Even so, *clearly delineated* is a problematic term. It projects something about our visual understanding of objects onto the much more nebulous term *experience*. But this only emphasises a very real dilemma—how to speak about experience, particularly non-objective or non-foundational experience. The effect on our experience when we use metaphors—or even the fact that certain metaphors exist in our culture—is not easy to grasp. One key way to understand the functioning of metaphor is with the notion that metaphors serve to highlight certain aspects of our experience while they downplay or hide other aspects. For example, some of the most pervasive metaphors underpinning Western culture at this time are entity and substance metaphors. We metaphorically project material existence and defined boundaries onto many phenomena. In many respects, this makes it easier to define and speak about them. Thoughts and ideas are a good example. We speak about them as though they are definite objects and this in turn can make aspects of them more definite in our experience; they may seem more lasting or more concrete. However, this also means that we do not attend to other aspects of these phenomena, such as their changeable, dynamic nature. The interesting point here is that *it seems* as though there is an experience to which we can attend and then understand differently—many people who have tried meditation will agree. But how much a different metaphor for thoughts or thinking changes the actual experience of it is not all that straightforward. Ideas, for example, may have a certain contained singularity about them when we attend to them that way or be much more amorphous and indistinct if we attend to them differently. Indeed the former might make them appear more real or important, and the latter less so. Lakoff and Johnson repeatedly raise this point. In *Philosophy in the Flesh* they ask, "Does the metaphor fit a pre-existing qualitative experience, or does the qualitative experience come from conceptualizing what we have done via that metaphor?"[5]

Many of the metaphors detailed by Lakoff and Johnson entail the projection of one highly structured concept onto another. In fact they say that most new metaphors that come into use are just that, the new metaphorical projections of one highly structured concept onto another. One example that Lakoff and Johnson discuss is *an argument is a battle*. Finding linguistic evidence for this metaphor is straightforward: we might *attack* another's point of view or *defend* our own. Our argument might be *shot down* or we might be *forced into a corner* so that we *surrender*. Once we understand *our position* we can *retreat* and *marshall our defences*. The whole concept of battle informs the concept of arguing not only in the way we speak about it. It encapsulates something important about both expected behaviour and the experience of arguing—the way an argument might play out, and the way participants might experience and respond within an argument. Lakoff and Johnson would say that such metaphors are not simply a matter of language, but that we *understand* arguing, at least partly or on some occasions, in this way. We metaphorically project some relevant yet holistic aspect of the structure of a battle onto an argument, and this gives us a sense of not only how to understand and describe what happens but might influence what actually happens and how we experience it. Of course—particularly for such a highly structured concept—this occurs within a specific cultural context. That the metaphor remains in use is a result of continuing social and cultural attitudes and values about arguing, which to an extent dictates what might happen.

Categorisation

Understanding how categorisation works in our conceptual system helps to clarify the functioning of metaphor. Categorisation is one of our most fundamental ways of making sense of the world. It allows us to organise our perceptions of objects and events by relating them to other objects and events. We generally think of categories as including the same kinds of objects or situations, by way of family resemblance (they all have something in common) based on something like a prototype (best example of a category, that may be entirely conceptual). Thus:

> Categories are neither fixed nor uniform. They are defined by prototypes and family resemblances to prototypes and are adjustable in context, given various purposes.[6]

This is easiest to comprehend in terms of objects. For example, we have general conceptual categories for many features of the natural world; trees, mountains, rivers, lakes. In our lives we encounter many different instances of, say, trees and different types of trees, and by also using the word *tree* across many different instances we form a prototype. The prototype might contain various features that trees usually have—say, a single trunk, branches and leaves—but remain a conceptual version of *tree*, which is a generalised version that doesn't actually physically exist anywhere. So in any given situation we can use the word *tree* and convey that to someone else, even if the actual trees we are referring to don't carry all the features of the prototype—such as pine trees, which have needles rather than leaves or palm trees which have no branches. The generalised version of the word *tree* will be enough in many situations, but not others in which more detail is required.

Categories of objects and events do not need to be seen as definitions that happen after perception. Rather, they may simply be the perception that is relevant to a given situation. This point relates to a view of perception as a process by which we differentiate from generalities rather than one where we add up details; a city dweller enjoying a drive through the countryside might simply see *trees*, while an environmentalist might see *invasive species of trees*. For the environmentalist the same kind of tree might be an *out-of-place menace* in a natural habitat and *a beautiful provider of greenery and shade* in an urban park. Categories are simply built in to our perceptions of things in particular contexts and for specific purposes. The only difference between categorisation and metaphor is that categories are projected onto what we usually think of as the same *kind* of thing whereas metaphors project from one domain, or *kind* of thing, to another. This is why those metaphors that project from the physical to the non-physical are perhaps the simplest to understand. Yet metaphor and categorisation are best seen as two ends of a continuum. Where one ends and the other begins is not always distinct.

Categories can also be goal-directed, which can mean that a category is formed of objects that may have nothing more in common than a purpose we have in mind. For example, planting trees is one way to reduce carbon in the atmosphere and slow climate change, but so is switching to electric cars, consuming less meat and voting for certain politicians over others. Of course, *purpose* generally refers to some action for a desired outcome, which opens up the potential for much more flexible and changeable categories than basic objects. Still, it is important to recognise that uniting objects or events according to purpose—as in goal-directed categories—does not mean that members of that category have nothing *real* in common. They may simply have nothing *physical* in common, if we understand purpose as something real.

Barrett discusses categories in relation to her view of emotions as concepts. Once again, because she finds no evidence for emotion fingerprints in the body, we need some other explanation as to how we understand emotions and can speak about them. Barrett sees emotions as prototypes we construct from diverse instances based on our goals, with our overriding goal being to regulate our body budgets—let's say, to maintain life and stability. According to Barrett, we construct these categories essentially through naming. Specific emotions have nothing physical in common but words offered in interactions prompt us—particularly as infants and children—to search for similarities across situations. She appears to be saying that some instances of emotion may have *nothing at all in common other than the word for them.* This means that she comes down very strongly on the side of social constructionism: "You are not finding similarities in the world but *creating* them."[7]

However, Barrett also says the following:

The newborn brain has the ability to learn patterns,
a process called *statistical learning*. The moment
that you burst into this strange new world as a baby,
you were bombarded with noisy, ambiguous signals
from the world and from your body. This barrage of
sensory input was not random: it had some
structure. Regularities.[8]

The notion of regularities doesn't fit well with a constructionist model. We need to understand much more about these regularities—beyond repeated words—and how they influence the maintenance of life and stability—or Barrett's body budget. One of the key claims of this book will be that there are regularities other than words that form our experiences of feeling, but that these are highly individualised—which makes speaking about emotion quite different from experiencing feeling. If emotions are learnt in situations, then when we name and speak about emotions we are perhaps more often than not speaking about behaviour or summarising situations. Nonetheless, individual experience of feelings can still be highly consistent. This may not make sense just yet, but should become clearer through this book.

The interesting parallel between Barrett's recent work and Lakoff and Johnson's *Metaphors We Live By* is the difficulty of characterising experience that is somehow conceptual but prior to language. It is also interesting that Lakoff and Johnson include experiences of emotion as less clearly delineated experiences, but not less basic. Their idea that we unconsciously use metaphorical projection to understand emotion—which presumably also influences our experience of emotion—will turn out to be a more powerful explanatory concept than emotions as goal-directed categories, in the context of constructionism. Barrett's view does make an important alignment between emotion and behaviour. Emotions as goal-directed categories implies action and purpose, which fits very well with a view of emotion as discernible in behaviour even if the feeling of an emotion is not occurring. However, Lakoff and Johnson's theory offers an important base because they avoid subjectivism (the idea that meaning is inherently subjective and relative) whereas Barrett's social constructionism combined with neuroscience ends up there, with an isolated brain in a skull.

Of course, I have still barely touched on the difference between emotion and feeling, because discussing this difference will be much simpler in the context of a different theoretical framework, which this book will develop. For now, it is worth simply pointing out an alignment between emotion and behaviour—better expressed as emotion and action—is in many ways consistent with Barrett's view of emotion. I will simply be saying in later chapters that feeling is something different again and is meaningful in a way that the body budget concept greatly impoverishes.

Regularities in experience

Simply because metaphors project from one domain to another does not mean that we can project any old concept onto some other realm of experience and make sense of it. Some will make sense and extend our understanding—and perhaps our experience—and some will not. At the same time, metaphorical projection takes place largely below conscious awareness. By highlighting and hiding, metaphor genuinely creates experience; it doesn't really make sense to refer to hidden experience. Again, this is difficult to understand if we only study language, and why a phenomenological perspective is so important in embodied cognition, and why much of the field of embodied cognition has involved applications of phenomenology.

Lakoff and Johnson posit two possible reasons for the existence of some metaphors rather than others; experiential co-occurrence and experiential similarity. These refer respectively to experiential events that happen at the same time or that are in some way similar. The metaphor *more is up* illustrates experiential co-occurrence; often in the physical world, when we see more of something we also see it increase in space, often upwards. We then project this pattern of the physical world onto other realms; "My bank balance is going up", or "You really need to study to raise your grades", or "Her self-esteem has skyrocketed since she won the competition". The metaphors *happy is up* and *sad is down* are also examples of experiential co-occurrence. Experiential similarity means there is something experientially—but not objectively—similar about the two phenomena, such as journeys and relationships, but this again raises the question of basic experience. For example, what is our *experience* of relationships before we understand it with other experiences via metaphor? Can we even meaningfully ask this question?

Lakoff and Johnson say that "There are many things we understand directly from our direct physical involvement as an inseparable part of our immediate environment".[9] Here, direct physical involvement implies unmediated experience, however Lakoff and Johnson are also quite clear that "all experience is cultural, through and through".[10] Usually we take the term culture to imply a specific kind—one among many possible cultures. While it may seem obvious, some kinds of direct physical engagement with an environment will be common to all humans because of the kinds of bodies we have. That we can name those as belonging to *human* culture rather than specific cultures is an important point. Of course, the ways that human kinds of engagement are elaborated upon in language and social interactions—in specific cultures and groups—can vary a great deal. For now, though, explicitly using the term *human culture* clarifies that we can speak about experience as being natural but not objective and unmediated. This provides an important link to the way that Lakoff and Johnson use the term *natural*, and to a phenomenological perspective of experience as both gestalt—or holistic—and structured.

They explain that

> *experiential gestalts are multidimensional*
> *structured wholes.* Their dimensions, in turn, are
> defined in terms of directly emergent concepts.
> That is, the various dimensions (participants,
> parts, stages, etc.) are categories that emerge
> naturally from our experience.[11]

In simpler terms, we might say that natural kinds of experience simply arise from being in a human body and interacting in a physical and social world. The dimensions that Lakoff and Johnson refer to are essentially the structure of the ways events tend to happen and the way things tend to appear to us. These dimensions seem to be strongly anchored in our physical experience of moving through the world and encountering situations. For instance, journeys are a natural kind of experience; they just happen in human lives. We simply get used to the sequence of moving our bodies through space. Stages are one of their natural dimensions—at their simplest: setting out, travelling and arriving. Thus, a holistic experience such as a journey involves dimensions that we can name but that are integral to it. The experience just arises but we can discern structure after the fact.

This way that both experience and understanding emerge in interaction—and are both naturally gestalt and naturally structured—is present in *Metaphors We Live By* but is better explained by further developments in embodied cognition, particularly Johnson's concept of *image schemata,* and by looking more closely at how enactivist theories complement and fill out the perspective so far explained. Even so, Lakoff and Johnson's original work in the stream of metaphor remains relevant in much of its detail. The linguistic evidence for the workings of conceptual metaphor is compelling and provides a clear path between objective and subjective versions of truth and reality. At the same time, much remains to be explored in the co-influence of experience and understanding—and how it arises in the first place, prior to language. The terms experience and understanding can also keep us anchored in usual life while considering more abstract ideas.

Image schemata as basic patterns

In *The Body in the Mind*, published seven years after *Metaphors We Live By*, Johnson deals with embodiment more directly and in more detail. He accounts for some of the experiences that form the basis for metaphorical projection with the concepts of basic-level and image schematic understanding. *Image schema*, in particular, is a concept that has continued through to more recent work. It describes a level of experience that gives "general form to our understanding in terms of structures".[12] The concept of image schemata characterises the sense of understanding and experience that emerges from repetitious and reliable interaction with the world—the way that meaning emerges from bodily experience. This meaning "exists as a continuous, analog pattern of experience and understanding".[13] Johnson discusses this at length in relation to our understanding and experience of physical force. We learn about different kinds of physical force— as repeatable patterns—simply by using and experiencing our bodies from the time of our birth. The patterns that emerge "are embodied and give coherent, meaningful structure to our physical experience at a *preconceptual* level, though we are eventually taught names for at least some of these patterns."[14] For example, *compulsion, attraction* and *blockage of movement* are names for some of the forces we encounter in usual life. Simply by experiencing the push and pull of different forces and observing the movement of objects we come to understand the natural structuring of these forces and form schemata for them.

We can interpret image schemata as a process of categorisation applied to situations and activity rather than objects. They "transcend any specific sense modality" and "involve operations that are analogous to spatial manipulation, orientation and movement."[15] Like metaphor, while these patterns are analog and gestalt—and are projected in a holistic way to understand other phenomena—they also have identifiable structure. This is much like Lakoff and Johnson's *dimensions* of experience. The structure usually involves parts (such as other people or objects) and relations (such as causal relations, sequences in time or location). Once again, this essentially describes an understanding of the way things tend to happen.

Similarly to the initial theory of metaphor, image schemata largely follow the theme of physical interaction to generate basic understanding. Much of Johnson's discussion is focused on physical—or sensorimotor—experience. As mentioned earlier, this is a general feature of the field of embodied cognition. In his more recent book, *The Meaning of the Body*, the theme of sensorimotor experience continues. Image schemata are seen to generate meaning from bodily experience: "The meaning is that of the recurring structures and patterns of our sensorimotor experience."[16] These patterns have a logic to them. Yet in this more recent work, Johnson anchors his theory in the work of the philosopher John Dewey, as part of a view of experience and understanding that is more dynamic and interactive. Even though the *structural* aspect of image schemata remains—which includes discussion of neural structures as *maps*—structure is not seen in isolation from a dynamic, living body interacting with an environment. Image schemata are described as neither mental nor bodily, but "as contours of what Dewey called the body-mind".[17]

Feeling is certainly mentioned in the initial theory of image schemata—as something like our sensibility of the arising of embodied patterns. Johnson even expresses the relation between these patterns and language in a similar way to Barrett:

> These embodied patterns do not remain private or
> peculiar to the person who experiences them. Our
> community helps us interpret and codify many of
> our felt patterns. They become shared cultural
> modes of experience and help to determine the
> nature of our meaningful, coherent understanding
> of our 'world'.[18]

In the more recent work, feeling gets a much more substantial discussion, as Johnson brings in a more phenomenologically oriented perspective to augment the theory of metaphor and concepts such as image schemata. This means a more direct attending to experience and its qualities—essentially *the feeling* of experience—as well as its context of arising from non-conscious bodily processes. Johnson is influenced by neuroscientist Antonio Damasio's theory, which understands emotion as related to responding in a situation, with feeling an experience that usually, but not always, follows.

Recall that within the theory of metaphor *emotions* are already understood and spoken about through metaphorical projection and that this projection should also influence experience, even if it is difficult to understand how. So *feeling*, then, as the perception of inner movements and fluctuations from the body is something different. Johnson includes some more direct descriptions of the full range of feeling:

> ...awareness of feeling falls along a continuum that
> runs from powerful passions that shake us to our
> core all the way to faint feelings of which we are
> only marginally, or even subliminally, aware.[19]

He also refers to some phenomenological concepts such as Eugene Gendlin's felt sense and Suzanne Langer's vitality-affect contours which are useful for describing feeling as *more than* and *different from* emotion.

At first glance, the difference here between emotion and feeling might not seem different from Barrett's. Feeling is basically affect, and when we have strong affect we might label this as emotion. However, for Barrett, affect is essentially meaningless and the act of labelling is where meaning is generated, whereas for Johnson, affect—or these vitality-affect contours, arising deeply from the body—is genuinely meaningful. Even though Johnson brings in a much more direct consideration of experience—which is a general theme of the continuing development of embodied cognition as a field—the relation between feeling and these basic structures of our experience (image schemata) remains difficult to understand. Our image schemata may have emotional salience in an ongoing dynamic situation but they are also operating below conscious awareness. This is why, he says, we need phenomenology (or to attend directly to our experience) but we must also go beyond it to understanding the non-conscious structuring of our experience.

I have discussed Lakoff and Johnson's early work and Johnson's more recent work in some detail for a few reasons. Firstly, much evidence has been gathered in support of their theory of metaphor. Johnson also reports that research in linguistics has shown the workings of image schemata in relation to many phenomena in many languages. Indeed *The Meaning of the Body* makes detailed references to empirical research from neuroscience and psychology as well as linguistics and philosophy; these are well-supported ideas. Secondly, I will build upon some of their concepts in this book, so it is important to present them from their original context, particularly for readers who may not know them.

Lastly, highlighting the trajectory of development of these concepts—even if they are explained here in a truncated and simplified form—shows how moving from the more traditional and dualistic view of mind and body in cognitive science towards a more embodied and dynamic perspective begins to require a different philosophical framework altogether. But that *feeling* remains not quite integrated into the theory suggests a need to further develop a framework. The theory, from the classic *Metaphors We Live By* though to Johnson's *The Meaning of the Body* states many times the need for a different philosophical framework. Johnson refers often to American pragmatist philosophy, and specifically to Dewey's work, as well as phenomenology. This book is an attempt to build a different framework, amenable to both pragmatism and phenomenology but also broader, to better explain feeling while maintaining a central place for metaphor.

3

Dynamic and structure

AN IMPORTANT THEME of the development of the theory of metaphor—and of embodied cognitive science more generally—is the ongoing peculiarity of attending to the wholeness or gestalt nature of experience while also keeping in mind its underpinnings by identifying structure.

> Experience comes whole and continuous. We make distinctions and abstract out patterns from this qualitative whole. On this view, cognition is an organic, embodied process of enaction in which the organism is dynamically engaged with its surroundings and is not separated or alienated from them.[1]

But something strange happens when we think of experience this way. The more that dynamic interaction comes to the fore, the more any kind of inwardness seems to recede or even disappear altogether. By inwardness I mean the personal nature of my experience. We can talk about experience generally and how it arises in interaction, but still there is the feeling of *my* body, *my* experience. At the same time, the more I emphasise this the more isolated the arising of *my* experience. This path can lead then to Barrett's isolated brain, cut off from the world, doomed to hypothesise and, essentially, hallucinate. We need instead to find a view that preserves inwardness but accommodates social reality and natural human experience. Natural means here both the way it was described earlier in relation to *human culture* but also the way that nature, found in evolutionary and developmental processes, makes living beings possible, beings at once dynamically engaged in and with the world and highly individuated. The nexus of all this must be feeling and the body—the gestalt and inward aspect of experience, and the living body. These should not be dualistically separated, but understood as perspectives on a single process unfolding over time, made possible only in the context of other processes unfolding over time.

Enactivism

These kinds of themes are strong in the enactivist approach to embodied cognition. In their classic text *The Embodied Mind*, Varela, Thompson and Rosch make definite statements about both this inwardness and outwardness of the body and experience, making reference to the philosopher Maurice Merleau-Ponty. They agree with Merleau-Ponty that embodiment has a "double sense" of "both the body as a lived, experiential structure and the body as the context or milieu of cognitive mechanisms".[2] They also make a clear and important statement that aligns with the way I have presented Lakoff and Johnson's work:

> The fundamental insight of the enactive approach
> as explored in this book is to be able to see our
> activities as reflections of a structure without losing
> sight of the directness of our own experience.[3]

They see a "deep tension in our present world between science and experience"[4] and offer that contemplative practices, such as those practised in Buddhist mindfulness meditation can provide an important counterpoint, as systematic inquiry into lived experience. This is essentially disciplined inquiry *from the inside*. They argue that without any process of inquiry other than the abstract attitude of science, nihilism is very difficult, perhaps impossible, to avoid. While *The Embodied Mind* is more than twenty-five years old—and mindfulness practices have become much more widespread in Western culture during this time—this problem remains as present as ever. In fact we can identify it in Barrett's theory. Her view of mind does resonate with Buddhist views; the hapless, endlessly guessing brain disconnected from a world is in some ways a similar theory of *no self*. She directly states: "My scientific definition of the self is inspired by the workings of the brain yet is sympathetic to the Buddhist view."[5] But Buddhism offers something completely different from the scientific approach, namely that the natural progression of inquiry will be to *something* (such as compassionate insight) rather than *nothing*. With Barrett's and many modern-day neuroscientific theories we simply end up alienated from ourselves and any sense of real meaning and value to be found in the world or in our experience. Conceptualising the self, as Barrett does, as "part of social reality"[6] doesn't really mitigate this.

Even so, two themes from Varela, Thompson and Rosch's early work seem to have been taken up much more within embodied cognitive science than serious applications of contemplative practices as part of theory making. The first theme, already mentioned, is a focus on action, particularly as inherent in processes of perception. The second is the influence of biology and systems theory.

Active engagement

With regard to perception—which has been most researched in relation to visual perception—action is understood as an inherent aspect of the whole process of perception and not separable from it. Our actions and interactions with the world and the way we are already engaged in any situation mean that visual perception is always for a purpose. This is similar to the functioning of conceptual categories mentioned earlier. We don't decode details of objects passively entering through the retina in our eyes and then reconstruct them in the brain. Rather, we make discriminations from a situation based on our needs in that situation, which are ultimately needs for action. They are ways we might proceed in a situation and enabled by our whole bodies and environments. Noë explains:

> Seeing is active. When you go to the theatre or a baseball game, you sit up and look around and move your eyes and your head; in this way you engage with the event in front of you. (Indeed, even when you try to be still, your eyes move on their own, making saccades three or four times a second.) Seeing is a kind of coupling with the environment, one that requires attention, energy and, most of the time, movement.[7]

Noë debunks two views that have underpinned vision science. One is the older view that we must explain how the brain recreates detailed, stable pictures of the world around us from poor retinal images, which are "tiny, discrepant, distorted, jumpy, upside-down, gappy, unevenly resolved, only partially colour sensitive [and] time delayed". The second, related view— which Noë terms the *new scepticism*—contends that we should explain how the brain makes us believe we have a detailed, stable picture of the world, when in fact we don't. Both position the brain as the master creator, and the second view, in particular, finds that the world is a *grand illusion*. Noë argues instead that retinal images are not the *data* for the experience of seeing; they are not what we need to explain. Rather, seeing emerges from our skillful involvement with a world that is actually there and "goverened by certain causal and physical regularities".[8] This focus on action challenges the boundaries between action, cognition and perception, as it also breaks down distinctions between brain, body and world in important ways.

Centralising action provides a way of understanding that

cognition is a form of dynamic contact with the world and not separable from the body. However, it can also emphasise continuity to the point where understanding, and perhaps experience, involves the world beyond the body in a counterintuitive way, as though brain, body and world form one undifferentiated system. Noë, for instance, remarks: "We ourselves are distributed, dynamically spread-out, world-involving beings."[9] Such a view emphasises the dynamic aspects of interacting rather than the structural aspects, which, from prior learning, make interaction possible. This also downplays the border of the body as relevant for consciousness.

Systemic adjustments

Even so, enactivism's shift to dynamic language is very important. In this regard Gallagher's recent *Enactivist Interventions* makes crucial inroads into profoundly changing how we can think about cognition and action. In comparison to predictive processing models of cognition, which have the brain making inferences and testing hypotheses as further sensory input arrives, enactivist explanations are simpler and more elegant. For example, Gallagher explains that "on the enactivist model the dynamic adjustment/attunement process that encompasses the whole of the system is not a *testing* that serves better neural prediction; active inference is not inference at all, it's a *doing*, an enactive adjustment, a worldly engagement".[10] This perspective makes it much easier to think in terms of a whole body engaging with the world, continuously attuning and refining responses through numerous complex *body and brain* processes that all influence each other. On this view "the brain is better conceived as participating in the action, enabling the system as a whole to attune to changing circumstances."[11] One of the main differences in these more dynamic explanations that no longer cast the brain as a central processing agent is, quite simply, *vocabulary* that is more suited to describing a living, active system—as opposed to terms that tend to reify dynamic processes.

Enactivist explanations draw much of this vocabulary from biology: "enactivists insist that biological aspects of bodily life, including organismic and emotion regulation of the entire body, have a permeating effect on cognition, as do processes of sensorimotor coupling between organism and environment."[12] Such whole body regulation in reciprocal causal relation with an environment is well described with reference to theories of self-organising systems.

The concept of emergence, for example, describes the observation that systems can cross thresholds such that new properties just occur, without the need to posit a separate, external causal agent. Emergence is a key concept in enactivism, described in some detail even in the early work by Varela, Thompson and Rosch. We can apply it to the development of Johnson's image schemata. Most of us have seen infants repeat certain movements and interactions, such as placing one object inside another then removing it, placing it back inside, then removing it. Let's say this is an aspect of the development of a *container* schema. At some point the infant has done this enough times that she simply understands that this happens when she manipulates certain objects in these ways. Of course many other experiences will contribute to understanding the basic logic of containment such as the experience of being inside the house or the car, and experiencing her own body as a container. Overall, the understanding generated can be seen as an instance of emergence. There is no separate internal director within her brain instructing this; it just happens as a result of these activities that involve the whole body and brain. We can imagine that there might be a physical and physiological description for how the system has changed—a holistic understanding has emerged from a repeated, sequenced activity—even if we don't know exactly what that is. But this will be description at a different level. It cannot *equal* the experience of understanding what a container is and how it works. While this is a simplified example, such explanations can make sense of how systems develop over time, generate novelty within themselves while continuously in dynamic contact with a changing environment.

Interestingly, this kind of language that suggests or directly refers to dynamic, complex systems is fairly commonplace in neuroscience, and Barrett also uses it. For example brain activity that generates emotion involves *cascades, dynamic constructions* and *storms of prediction*. But, aside from some small fields such as enactivism and theoretical biology, such language often seems to be used without a strong and explicit explanation of how systems function and what the implications are, in terms of basic assumptions about the world and metaphors that are consistent with these. If we continue to fall back on the idea of the brain as an isolated agent—which, as said is also prevalent in neuroscience, even in the more complex and dynamic predictive processing models—we simply lose ground in our overall understanding of how cognition happens. Even the term *cognition* seems overly separated, which is why the terms *experience* and *understanding* were used at length earlier; they make room for broader views. Explanations of the development and functioning of systems, as well as the philosophical principles that underlie these, should simply give us a foundation for more descriptive and consistent metaphors. The applications of these in understanding feeling and the body could be far-reaching because they could change our ideas about the meaning and value of human life, possibly even life altogether.

Of course, theorising feeling and the body through some of the ideas already presented and in a philosophical context should help to situate the theories discussed. The point here is to develop underlying theory rather than to disagree with empirical research, which Barrett's view of emotion, the theory of metaphor and the enactivist perspective are all well supported

CONTEMPORARY PERSPECTIVES

by. The purpose also is not to claim that the brain doesn't have any special functions. Rather, these need to be kept in perspective, as neural processes made possible by and in reciprocal relation to other processes. Some research in neuroscience appears to be heading that way, particularly in relation to the role of interoception and homeostasis. The neuroscientist Antonio Damasio develops a perspective on this in his most recent book *The Strange Order of Things*. He provides a vital perspective on feeling and the body—particularly in relation to the brain—that augments all those already discussed. Damasio's previous work on brain and body relations is also an important support for the primacy of action put forward by the enactivists, as well as the relation between emotion and action.

Damasio on feeling and the body

Damasio explores the emergence of consciousness in individuals, and cultures in societies, through the themes of feeling and homeostasis. He outlines an expanded view of homeostasis, which links directly to all forms of biological life:

> Homeostasis is the powerful, unthought, unspoken
> imperative, whose discharge implies, for every
> living organism, small or large, nothing less than
> enduring and prevailing.[13]

Feelings are essentially the subjective experience of this, "of the state of life—that is, of homeostasis—in all creatures endowed with a mind and a conscious point of view."[14] Rather than limiting homeostasis to the more narrow definition of maintaining a steady, balanced state necessary for survival, Damasio presents homeostasis as oriented towards flourishing as well as health and stability. It has a natural direction that is conducive to the development of future wellbeing. This allows him to say that *feeling* is the impetus for the development of cultures. Cultures, or social, minded processes, provide the means to intervene in individual, biological processes. Cultures develop ways to regulate and improve human lives.

Building on his previous work, Damasio places feeling in the context of evolutionary development. This provides a link between feeling and the sensing and responding to an environment present in simpler forms of life such as bacteria. The development of multicellular life brings ever more refined modes of sensing an environment, along with greater inner differentiation; the development of organs and systems within organisms. Importantly, the more complex biological interiors of organisms eventually require more sophisticated means of coordination, initially chemical and later neural:

> The coordination was provided by the endocrine
> system via chemical molecules known as hormones
> and by the immune system, which ensured
> inflammatory responses and immunity. The master
> global coordinators followed suit. They were, of
> course, the nervous systems.[15]

In some ways we can loosely identify a similar narrative to Barrett's, in the focus on the link between homeostasis and feeling—or, in Barrett's case, emotion—and its further regulation by cultural processes. Indeed, Damasio's metaphor here of nervous systems as master global coordinators might also be seen as commensurate with Barrett's perspective, and most of neuroscience. Damasio uses the term *surveillance* as a metaphor for interoception, which he also terms visceroception because so much information about the state of life in the conscious organism comes from the viscera (the organs, blood and smooth muscle). He describes interoception as tiered, with a level that is unconscious and can make regulatory adjustments in the body, and a level that is conscious and produces subjective states of feeling. Surveillance, or interoception, as he sees it, does allow for anticipation and prediction, but also for "straightforward information" about the state of the body.[16] Thus, interoception is a genuinely receptive as well as predictive process.

Damasio emphasises the evolutionary development of interoception from earlier neural structures that were directly acted upon by chemical molecules in the blood—thus, stronger reciprocal relations between chemical and neural signalling. He describes the increased separation between these two types, forming more and more distinct systems. Damasio then names (in evolutionary terms) the *old interior* of the viscera and the *new interior* of the bony skeleton, skeletal muscle and sensory portals (eyes, ears, etc.). The new interior receives information from and maps changes in the old interior; "These images of the old internal world are none other than core components of *feelings*."[17] The visceral, old interior is identified with chemical signalling and homeostasis and the new interior with the specialised senses and voluntary movement. Thus, the new interior is oriented both inwards, to the state of the viscera and outwards, through body movement and the sense organs. Importantly the new interior also has a protective function.

> the vulnerabilities of the new internal world are
> smaller than the old. The skeleton and the
> skeletal musculature form a protective carapace.
> It sturdily envelops the tender old world of
> chemistries and viscera.[18]

But Damasio is also careful to describe the direct interactions between chemical and neural that continue to exist in the body. These occur in areas without a blood-brain barrier; in some areas of the ventricles (fluid filled spaces) in the brain, as well as in the *dorsal root ganglia*. These ganglia (bunches of nerves) are located along the spinal column and link peripheral nerves with the spinal cord. They are where body signals are conveyed to the central nervous system. The lack of blood-brain barrier here means that the neurons do convey peripheral signals but, at the same time, "they are modulated *directly* by molecules circulating in the blood".[19] Furthermore, interoceptive signals from the body are mostly conveyed via nerve fibres that lack myelin—a coating that acts as insulation, supporting faster, more efficient signal transmission. This coating is present on nerve fibres that convey information about the external world from the special senses (eyes, ears, skin) but not from the interior body. Homeostasis, then, "is in the hands of the electrically leaky, slow, and ancient unmyelinated fibers",[20] which are much more open to their surrounding chemical environments than the newer, myelinated fibres.

Even with increasingly complex internal separation for coordination, areas of greater integration persist, and more and more of these integrations are being uncovered in research.[21] Furthermore, the part of the nervous system that surveys and responds to the old interior "has always worked cooperatively with the immune and endocrine system within that same interior".[22] This suggests that separation between systems is more graded and systems more blended than we ordinarily assume or even know about yet. The enteric nervous system (in the gut) is also outside of the usual brain and body separation. Most of its hundreds of billions of neurons function intrinsically (meaning that they communicate among themselves), suggesting much greater internal regulation from within itself as a separate structure than direction from the brain. Interestingly, Damasio suggests the name *first* brain for the enteric nervous system, more evolutionarily accurate than the popular term *second* brain.

Given such complexity of integration and separation, it appears that Damasio doesn't actually view the brain or nervous system as master controller or ultimate regulator. In fact he describes the nervous system as, historically, an *assistant* or "a servant of whole-organism homeostasis".[23] He sees the relation between brain tissue and the body as key in understanding the emergence of feeling and consciousness and, eventually, culture, creativity and intelligence. He remarks that "this integrated mutuality is most often overlooked in discussions of behaviour and cognition".[24]

Damasio's perspective on the importance of neural structures beyond the brain, places where the body and nervous system are functionally blended, and whole body systems and relationships in understanding consciousness and feeling aligns well with the enactivist perspective. The important counterpoint that Damasio's work brings is his emphasis on the strong boundary between the individual organism and the surrounding environment. There is much more dynamic activity and communication going on within an organism than between it and an environment. This is present in the enactivist perspective; organisms as living systems manifesting operational closure is certainly a key aspect of enactivism. But, as already mentioned, it is minimised when present time dynamic interaction in an environment is emphasised. Damasio's view maintains the private, inward nature of feeling in the context of the organism as a complex system, and imbues it with real meaning. This meaning may be likened to immanent meaning that just emerges from activity, as with the development of image schemata—meaning that is experientially real but not objective or unmediated. In this context, how conscious experience arises from processes that are not conscious is a key issue. Damasio's focus on feeling also augments the enactivist approach where it has tended to focus heavily on sensory-motor activity but less on feeling. Gallagher also notes this "neglect of the relevance of affective aspects of embodiment". He states that "Bodily activity... involves a complex ensemble of factors that govern conscious life."[25]

A hierarchical model of consciousness

In earlier work, Damasio describes the emergence of consciousness and the emergence of a self using models of hierarchical organisation, consistently placing emotion at the level of complex action that precedes awareness and feeling as an emergent level of consciousness. If we understand that action is always for a purpose—in the expanded sense of flourishing, even in simpler organisms—*and* that action need not require awareness or consciousness then we can simplify the difference between emotion and feeling. Emotion is a class of action with strong purpose. Damasio lists emotions "in the more conventional sense of the term" among the causes of feeling, and describes emotions as "action programs activated by confrontation with numerous and sometimes complex situations."[26] These may give rise to certain kinds of feeling, but feeling encompasses a much broader range of experience. The key to understanding feeling is that it is ubiquitous but "often so subtle that it does not demand attention for itself".[27]

One of the reasons for this subtlety of feeling is that we are often not attuned to it. Rather, we are attuned outwardly, with our attention often taken up by the world as the setting for our more or less habitual actions, by languaged thoughts and interactions, or both at the same time. But this higher level, language—or *extended* consciousness, in Damasio's terms[28]—emerges from the lower level of feeling. Feeling is not a report back to the brain from the body, even if it functions *on some level* as information for what comes next. Nor is it a by-product of the brain's instructions to the body. It is the holistic emergence of conscious awareness that makes other, so-called *higher* forms of consciousness possible. While it has a quality of being within an organism or a human being, it is the experience of a whole body and always in relation to an environment. Of course, feeling changes and differentiates over time, and particularly through development, and naming experiences does influence and refine this process. But, as with the way concepts emerge and extend metaphorically, differentiated feeling does simply arise through repetitive types of activity and interaction.

Damasio's work is interesting and often breaks new ground because he is very much of a biological (or neurobiological) perspective but he also directly faces feeling in the phenomenological sense of experience. As with Lakoff and Johnson, Damasio's work features the concept of representation as *neural maps*, although he focuses more on interoceptive maps of the body that can stand in for the actual body in other cognitive processes. This fits quite well with Johnson's image schemata. But the term representation continues to carry unclear and objectivist connotations, well summarised by Gallagher, who describes it as "an awkward place-holder for an explanation that still needs to be given in dynamical terms of an embodied, environmentally embedded and enactive model."[29] Shifting the language around representation might make it less problematic, although as Gallagher also mentions, alternate, non-representational explanations might make the concept redundant. Even if summary forms of understanding have a causal relationship to patterns of neural events, they must also have a causal relationship to a living body in a changing environment. Such patterns—which are a feature of Barrett's view of prediction as essentially dynamic—cannot be sensibly spoken about outside the context of a body and experience, all of which is highly patterned and has developed over time, both in an individual and the evolution of a species. In terms of experience, feeling and other kinds of conscious awareness that seem more controllable, such as abstract thinking or imagining, need to be understood both in their phenomenal aspects (how they appear in awareness) and in the world in which they arise and are deeply related to.

But all that I have said so far requires much more

explanation. For example, I have referred to hierarchical organisation without explaining it. All of the authors so far discussed also at some point refer, either directly or implicitly, to hierarchical organisation, a model of causal interaction that has explanatory power in complex systems. However its causal principles are not always carried through and the deeper implications of it as a way of looking at the physical world are discussed even less. This book will explain some of these principles and how they can help to make sense of living systems in a way that positions experience and understanding in relation to the physical and phenomenal world. These ideas help to generate a theory of a self—human and individual—that is both stable and real but deeply relational. This, in turn, supports a view of feeling as highly individualised but systematic and sensible in ways we usually overlook in everyday life, and as a separate phenomenon from emotion, which is better identified with purposeful action. The concept of metaphor, understood as both dynamic and structure, will help to organise this view of feeling.

A broader philosophical explanation that can make all of these phenomena more comprehensible demands that we move beyond either/or distinctions between subjective and objective. It is as much about new uses of language as about new ideas. If these kinds of language, and the ideas that support them, are developed so that they come into more general use then some of the discrepancies among theories could very well disappear. In *Enactivist Interventions*, Gallagher presents the enactivist model of embodied cognition as a philosophy of nature, one which should both respond to and challenge science. This book aims to generate interdisciplinary theory, but will present speculative naturalism and process metaphysics as a base. It is not in the tradition of enactivism as such but is very much in line with this aspect of the enactivist project. But the purpose overall is not so much to explain cognition as to show that feeling is central to human life in a way that we—if we follow the dominant neuroscientific paradigm—no longer seem to understand or appreciate. Some of the biggest differences among the theories discussed in these opening chapters are where feeling, even consciousness, is placed, in terms of both its role and its importance. The differences by which we then frame these theories have enormous implications for the way we see ourselves and live our lives; feeling as the quintessential experience of being alive or as the by-product of an instrumentalising brain; as full of meaning or bereft of it; as ever-present, tangible *and* mysterious or as only of functional, survival value. These differences matter much more than the language of neuroscience can cope with.

PART 2

THEORIES OF NATURE

4

Beyond the dynamics of dualism

FEELING IS DIFFICULT TO EXPLAIN. This is evident in the intricacies and inconsistencies of all the theories already discussed. It is at the heart of the problem of understanding the relation between mind and body. While our ability to observe physical processes (not least neural processes) continues to advance, we still cannot fathom the relationship between consciousness and these processes—or consciousness and the physical world in general. We seem genuinely trapped in a dualistic mode of thinking.

Even so, it is not immediately obvious for whom this dualism is a problem. Many neuroscientists, for example, work under the tacit assumption that advances in our technical ability to observe neural processes, along with the accumulation of detailed knowledge of such processes, will eventually explain the relation between mind and body. Thus, all will eventually be explained in terms of physical processes and dualism is not a deep conceptual problem. In philosophy this view is commonly known as materialism. An interesting extension of a materialist perspective is the idea that when this happens, when we have mapped all the details of human brains, the field of psychology will become redundant. Neuroscience will eclipse psychology. Yet this is only one example of a materialist point of view. A biologist more interested in broader physiological processes might believe that these, along with neural processes, will eventually generate a full description of mind.

At the complete other end of the spectrum, many people hold religious or spiritual beliefs that a transcendent force existed before and continues to pervade the physical world.

Some people living more secular lives even invoke beliefs about transforming the physical world with their own minds. Such beliefs in transcendent realities tend to also render the relation between mind and body unimportant; some kind of god-mind, collective intelligence or individual mind is the ultimate explanation for everything. This view is known in philosophy as idealism. While materialism and idealism have conceptual roots in ancient Greek philosophy, their modern forms are relatively recent in the history of Western thought.[1]

Materialism and Idealism

Many people in contemporary Western societies identify as believing in materialism—the idea that the physical world is what basically exists and minds are wholly dependent upon and can be explained in terms of it. This is probably the view of many working scientists, with the exception of physicists. But many people with a professional or personal interest in science will nonetheless see the relation between mind and body as a genuine conceptual problem, either for science or philosophy or both. Even if we live by the view that science generates objective knowledge about the physical world and everything that exists is basically physical matter (a materialist belief) if we recognise that the mind-body problem exists in a deeper way than will be solved simply by adding more detail, we are effectively questioning materialism. Of course many people maintain religious or spiritual beliefs while also seeing science as an accurate description of the physical world, and might understand the mind in relation to these spiritual beliefs. But for those whose lives are entirely secular, consideration of the mind-body problem may also simply reflect an aim to understand the natural duality in our experience of our own minds and bodies— between the apparently inward, phenomenal nature of our experience as distinct from our outward, physical bodies.

Many nuanced philosophical positions may be taken in relation to materialism and idealism, and the dualism they arose from, and many different accounts of their cultural and philosophical development are possible. The philosophical biologist Hans Jonas (whose book *The Phenomenon of Life* was published in 1966) provides an expansive narrative of the history of dualism. He discusses its development in relation to perceptions of life and death as experienced through the body, beginning with premodern thought. People in premodern times were more likely to observe the pervasive presence of life in the world. Life itself was ubiquitous and people struggled to make sense of mortality, to solve "the riddle of death".[2] However this orientation towards life changed with scientific advancements during the Renaissance and leading into the scientific revolution. Modern thought eventually became the complete opposite; making sense of life became the challenge.

One major change, often attributed to the scientist Francis Bacon (1561-1626), concerned the way nature was investigated; the new *method* of science. According to this new approach, the best way to gain knowledge and understand nature was to manipulate and dissect the physical world, relying on experimentation and impartial observation. It assumed that sense perceptions provided an objective perspective. Nature eventually became understood as inanimate masses and forces operating according to laws—as a machine made of essentially dead matter. This reductionist method and the correlate mechanical view of the world was incredibly successful in developing our knowledge and understanding of *some aspects* of the natural world, certainly how we might manipulate nature to our human ends. Yet this view of nature made life itself difficult, even impossible, to explain.

Death is the natural thing, life the problem. From
the physical sciences there spread over the
conception of all existence an ontology whose
model entity is pure material, stripped of all
features of life.[3]

The concepts of objective observation and dead matter
resulted in a more radical separation of observer and observed,
subject and object than had come before—a more complete
dualism than its predecessor in Greek philosophy. This version
of dualism was epitomised in the philosophy of René Descartes
(1596-1650) and remains pervasive in Western culture.

However, Jonas explains that changes in religion were
equally, if not more important to the development of modern
dualism as the rise of science and its rigorous investigation of
nature. He describes the discovery of the *self*, which began in
Orphic (ancient Greek) religion but culminated in the
recognition in Christian and Gnostic religion of "an entirely
nonmundane inwardness in man".[4] Jonas means here that more
and more emphasis was placed on the *inner life*, the human soul,
and its "complete foreignness"[5] with respect to nature or the
world. Thus, it is important to recognise that the development of
modern dualism in science reflected and reinforced
developments in religion. The universe of essentially dead
matter could only be animated by a transcendent god. Similarly,
the essentially dead body must be animated by a transcendent
mind or soul.

The more complete split between self and world, mind and
nature—which was "long sanctioned by religious doctrine"[6] and
then *reinforced* by scientific developments—made the views of
materialism and idealism possible. These views are *monisms*.
They are metaphysical positions that explain reality with
reference to a single phenomenon, either matter or mind. The
important point to grasp is that these perspectives only occur in
relation to the dualism that preceded them, which is why Jonas

sees "the rise and long ascendancy of dualism"[7] as so pivotal in Western history. Eventually the success of science paved the way for a complete determinism that had no need for the invisible workings of god.

> Accordingly, it is the existence of life within a mechanical universe which now calls for an explanation, and explanation has to be in terms of the lifeless.[8]

We should take note of the historical trajectory of these ideas because it highlights that materialism is really only part of the story. Materialism gives up the presence of life as something that should be central to any explanation of the world in which we find ourselves. Even with conceptual advances in so many fields of science, particularly those exploring complex systems and emergent properties, explanations remain limited by materialism as one side of a discontinuity. It is very difficult, probably impossible, to create satisfactory explanations for complex phenomena from materialism alone. This is why the metaphor of the machine, central to the development of science, has given way to the metaphor of the computer in much of neuroscience. The brain remains a machine, but now just a more complex one. When the relation between this complex machine and the mind is faced and named by philosophers the result is simply another dualism.[9]

Tending towards the opposite

Identifying that materialism, as a concept, relies on the pre-existing dualism clarifies aspects of Barrett's work that render some of her interpretations confusing. It explains why it contains a mix of perspectives. In Barrett's formulation emotions are, importantly, released from the more deterministic, classical view that specific emotions occur when fairly fixed patterns of physiological change are triggered. Barrett doesn't find a consistent match between our labels for specific emotions and specific changes in physiology, facial expression or neuronal firing patterns. Thus she finds that our experience cannot be explained in purely physical terms, which is why she suggests that emotions are concepts and socially constructed. She then suggests that we can change our experience by substituting concepts, such as interpreting anxiety as excitement. Even though the socially constructed concepts are ultimately described as brain processes—which we usually imagine in physical terms, even if they are complex and dynamic—experience ends up having not much to do with the physical. Experience is then described with statements that could easily be read as idealist, such as that "you are an architect of your experience".[10]   When the irreducibility of human experience to physical processes points to the need for new explanations these explanations tend towards the opposite (idealism) because the dualism is already implied in the materialist assumptions of the science that we begin with. There simply aren't other positions available. This reveals that the conceptual change required to better describe and understand experience and its relation to the body must occur in the most fundamental concepts through which we understand the world. We must move beyond this initial dualism.

A dynamic of flipping to the extreme opposite view, from materialism to idealism, when new explanations are sought exists more broadly in contemporary Western culture. In fact we can identify this dynamic in the development of the field of psychology. Psychology was made possible by the prior existence of the scientific method of experimentation and impartial observation, but it turns towards human experience rather than the outward nature of the physical world. However, an equally important precondition was, as mentioned earlier, the very notion of a self, of the inner life as separate and important, which developed through Christianity. William James (1842-1910), whose work is highly cited in introductions to the topics of emotion and feeling, is widely regarded as the founder of psychology. Sigmund Freud (1856-1939), born little more than a decade later, was the founder of psychoanalysis. Both James' ideas about psychology and emotion, and Freud's theories of the self, including concepts such as the unconscious, have had an enormous influence on our psychological views. Some have found their way into our everyday life and remain current in contemporary Western culture.

Importantly, these two grand thinkers in psychology developed highly influential ideas in the late nineteenth and early twentieth century, also a period of increasing secularisation. Indeed both Freud and James wrote about religious experience as personal feeling.[11] Thus, psychology developed (at least in part) where a gap emerged in ideas about the meaning of human life. The religious or spiritual import of the inner life or human soul was being questioned and explored. It makes sense that the close study, in the style of science, of inner life would follow. The replacement however—materialism directed at experience—was essentially *no meaning*. This is the nihilism that Varela, Thompson and Rosch mention as the endpoint for science as the only mode of inquiry.

In his book *The Triumph of the Therapeutic* (published in the same year as *The Phenomenon of Life*, in 1966) Philip Rieff describes this switch in attitudes to human life by way of the development of psychoanalysis in the context of the scientific method. He distinguishes between two types of theory. The first, prior to the scientific revolution, did not see knowledge, meaning and value as separate: "Theoretical knowledge is therefore of the good; the ideal is the most real."[12] The idea behind this is that an order of things exists and we can discover it, which not only tells us how things are (knowledge), but our place in the universe and how we should live (meaning and value). The attitude of science, however, did not struggle to find the way things are so that we might *conform* to this reality, to find some way to live in harmony with a natural order or seek direction, solace or reassurance. Rather, science seeks knowledge of nature only so that we might *transform* nature to our own ends. This knowledge tells us nothing about ultimate ends; it is completely bereft of value. Therefore, "theory becomes actively concerned with mitigating the daily miseries of living rather than with a therapy of commitment to some healing doctrine of the universe".[13]

Transforming the inner life

In the context of mechanistic and reductionist science attempting to find explanations for the inner life that could replace the idea of a separately existing human soul, the individual human being is the natural unit of explanation. Thus, in historical and theoretical terms, psychology attempts a scientific explanation of the individual self. Therapeutically, psychology tends to uphold improving life as an important goal. In relation to improving the inner life, feeling and emotion are obviously important, even central. However, as a *science*, psychology must uphold the same ideology; improvement must mean increased control over nature, in this case the nature of the inner life. Put simply, psychology should help us to feel better by increasing our power over the inner life by means of interventions. Rieff puts it this way: "the aim of psychoanalysis is the aim of science-power; in this case a transformative technology of the inner life."[14]

These are somewhat abstract points and not necessarily the way ordinary people in Western culture see things or live their lives, whether they use the interventions of psychology or not. However, as an underlying ideology the directive of gaining power over nature in an essentially meaningless universe remains central and powerful. The modern Western self generated in this context is a disconnected individual who can only seek more; "The reformer only asks for more of everything —more goods, more housing, more leisure; in short, more life."[15] The fact that this doesn't work, that the inner life is not transformed in the right way, that people don't, ultimately, feel better is evident in the high levels of mental ill health, anxiety, depression and dependence on pharmaceutical interventions in Western countries, despite unprecedented levels of wealth and longevity; and with these conditions not limited to those who are missing out on the wealth.[16]

Interestingly, the years since both Jonas and Rieff published their books have only seen the desire for more (which Rieff terms the *appetitive mode*) increase to reach fever pitch. Science as a way of seeing and investigating the world has only become stronger, with advances in neuroscience arguably taking centre stage. As this has happened, however, a parallel enormous increase in the use of complementary therapies and esoteric spiritualities has occurred, perhaps as attempts to fill the gaps in meaning and value in secular life.[17] Most interesting, though, is that when people seek different explanations for their lives or ways of coping, the answers are often, once again, the opposite in the dualism. The power of the mind to transform experience—which underlies the field of psychology, at least to an extent—is emphasised until it flips over into idealism. Hence, the narratives of controlling the physical world with the mind (popularly known as *manifesting*) have increased alongside rapid advancements in science and technology.[18] Even if the individuals who believe in either science or manifesting tend to be different, these two opposite views exist side-by-side in contemporary culture, with plenty of adherents to each (and some odd combinations). Tellingly, it is not much of a jump from the view of the hallucinating brain to the idea that any reality can be created. This shows up the dynamic of dualisms, that ideas eventually tend towards their opposites.

Discussing such long and complicated cultural changes in simple terms is difficult. It may be misleading to even try to generalise about what scientists or psychologists think or practice. Neither are unified fields and a multitude of approaches exist. At the same time, as fields of the development of knowledge, certain specific changes in ideas do occur and remain strong and relevant, and the dynamics among different ideas are important to at least try to describe. Descriptions of shifts in the ideas and directives that guide cultures and societies cannot capture the dynamic lived details of the development of so many lives, groups, institutions etc. But basic changes in understanding do demonstrate a genuine structure, even if we identify it after the fact—in the same way that metaphors were described as exhibiting both dynamic and structure. There is a deep, underlying structure in the way we think about things; about ourselves, each other and nature. The idea that people are essentially disconnected individuals responsible for themselves, for example, permeates almost every facet of contemporary Western culture. The attitude toward nature as of no inherent value and there for our use becomes an attitude toward inner nature in the context of the psychological self. We see this in the idea that feeling is an essentially meaningless by-product of a physical brain whose only imperative is to sustain physical life. We may as well change feeling in any way we can to something more pleasant, because (in this view) it carries neither inherent value nor genuine understanding.

The need for a shift

This discussion hopefully shows that getting beyond dualism is not merely a theoretical endeavour. As Damasio rightly points out, feeling is the basis of our sense of meaning and this drives every aspect of our culture. When we think about feeling in this way—as the basis of inner life in all its nuances and involved in our sense of the meaning of anything—it is easier to distinguish from emotions. Emotions are particular and much more narrow types of responding and more akin to acting.

Of course there is no point returning to an apparently lost sense of oneness, to the "integral monism of prehistory"[19] mentioned by Jonas. We are in and of this culture and need to work with the successes and failures of the way it has developed. Furthermore, Jonas contends:

> dualism had not been an arbitrary invention, for the two-ness which it asserts is grounded in reality itself. A new integral, i.e. philosophical monism cannot undo the polarity; it must absorb it into a higher unity of existence from which the opposites issue as faces of its being or phases of its becoming. It must take up the problem which originally gave rise to dualism.[20]

There is also no need to denounce any of the discoveries of science or condemn the practices of science, only to show where the limits are. Even if some of the practices and theories of science have moved well beyond the initial mechanistic and reductionist orientation—and for some, such as physics, this happened one hundred years ago—an overall materialist orientation remains. Even more entrenched are the metaphors that have extended into everyday usage which often lag behind changes in theoretical fields—metaphors that, for example, see the body as a machine and the individual as a disconnected entity. Similarly, psychology, as a science and as a therapy, need not be rejected. But the way that the ideology of science justifies attitudes towards people must be pointed out. With only the directive of science and the inner life no longer understood in the context of religious or spiritual faith, any meaning other than feeling good is hard to find. In Rieff's words, "Psychological man is born to be pleased".[21] This might explain the way that the boundaries blur from psychology to self-help to idealist views of attracting the good life. They all serve the same function; pleasing the individual.

It is interesting that when we trace the historical development of new ideas (particularly in overviews such as this one) we often present the major thinkers as though the new ideas originated wholly with them. For example we attribute the scientific method to Francis Bacon, and the mind-body split (known as Cartesian dualism) to René Descartes. In reality an entire and complex set of preconditions made their lives and innovations possible. This is not to deny that genuine creativity and singular innovations are possible, but to suggest that, usually, a major shift in thinking will be preceded by all sorts of rumblings—theoretical, social, cultural—until something finally gives way and a given individual or group is poised to fulfil the change, even if the way they do so is in itself highly creative. This concept of change is well known in the philosophy of science. In *The Structure of Scientific Revolutions,* Thomas Kuhn describes how such dynamics occur within science and lead to paradigm shifts.[22]

The difficulty of characterising experience, particularly feeling, as discussed in the opening chapters of this book, is indicative of the need for a paradigm shift. The clear statements that Lakoff and Johnson, and Varela, Thompson and Rosch make about the limitations of the belief in impartial, objective knowledge of a purely material world show that the theoretical rumblings began more than twenty-five years ago. Both of these texts were major contributions to a new field of inquiry in cognitive science. A concern with embodiment, or the living body, is also evident in Damasio's work and the inconsistencies in the role of the body in Barrett's work portend the need for a fundamental shift. This shift has already been named, at a conceptual level, as getting beyond the division between subjective and objective. Theorising feeling and the living body is one facet of this overall shift. Understanding inner life is related to the problem of understanding life itself, a problem that is not well handled by materialism.

It is useful to think of feeling in terms of both the sense of life and the sense of meaning—not the meaning of life in the grand sense, but how the mundane, lived sense of both life and meaning are the basis of our experience, our conscious life. If we can understand feeling in a new way it could help us to more genuinely and fully appreciate life. This includes life in the simple sense of our own lives but also a broader context of life generally. A much deeper appreciation of life is a key step towards the kind of care that is required for new ways of relating to nature. In this way, and at its best, new ways of understanding life could indeed offer some kind of new "healing doctrine of the universe" that gives us a stronger sense of what matters in these times. We might discover an *inbuilt ethical direction* for healing individuals, communities and the natural world, without relying on appeals to supernatural forces or beliefs in the oneness of mind. We could extend beyond the simple notion of *feeling good* as a goal to encourage the kind of flourishing that supports more stable forms of happiness and a good life, including harmony within and between people.

As a broader theory should preserve the insights of the sciences, including psychology, it should also preserve the gains in tolerance and diversity of the late twentieth and early twenty-first century. These were brought about in part by challenging power structures and celebrating subjectivity. Post-modernism in the humanities legitimised a plurality of perspectives and voices, which had very real effects on the rights of many minority groups. But post-modernism also ushered in an era in which knowledge became understood as relative. This stance makes collective problem solving difficult and can even make truth seem inconsequential, an attitude that is currently playing out in public affairs and social media. However, as the global problems of our time attest, we humans are very much in the same boat. Thus, the ideas that take us beyond the extremes of subjective and objective should also help to generate a narrative of connectedness. Understanding how consciousness and feeling arise in the context of natural processes needs to make sense of the ways we are both highly individuated and strongly interconnected beings, firstly with each other and more broadly with all of life, the life that is central to this world.

Of course we are also, unavoidably, psychological beings. We are concerned with our own feelings and our individual lives. But a better understanding of feeling in general can provide the means to understand our interconnectedness. The systematic and rigorous investigation of nature *does* free us from many of our illusions, but not the illusion that we are separate individuals who ultimately benefit from exploiting each other and the natural world.

5

Speculative philosophy and a new naturalism

IDENTIFYING THE FOUNDATIONAL BELIEFS of dualism, and then materialism and idealism, seems to go two ways. We can see them as both philosophical abstractions from and genuine commentaries and influences on culture and history. This points to an important role of philosophy as a discipline, a role that has been in decline through the late twentieth and into the twenty-first century. Academic philosophy has historically been much more concerned with systems of knowledge than it tends to be today. In universities nowadays philosophy is largely made up of sub-fields such as philosophy of mind, ethics, political philosophy, logic and so on, and then numerous sub-fields and specialisations within these. Philosophy that is concerned with systems of knowledge however, tries to do almost the opposite. It deals with the most basic concepts that orient world-views; our fundamental ideas about what exists and how we can know things. As a branch of philosophy, this is often termed *metaphysics* but a better term (which is not well known because this type of philosophy is not very common) is *speculative philosophy*.

Speculative philosophy aims to uncover basic assumptions about the world and their ramifications, to then suggest alternatives and follow through their implications. Thus, this type of philosophy is genuinely speculative; it tests ideas. However, it does not do this in a vacuum. It takes up the problems of culture and history, including the problems of science. Even more importantly, speculative philosophers seek to be highly systematic and produce internally consistent systems. In this way it can be on a par with science and offers an important counterpoint to scientific inquiry, particularly empirical research.

In his recent book *Philosophical Foundations of Ecological Civilization*, Arran Gare discusses the method for speculative philosophy, first outlined by the philosopher C.D. Broad (1887-1971).[1] Broad published during the period in which speculative philosophy was eclipsed by analytic philosophy, a philosophy that continues to dominate the Anglo-American tradition. As is evident in its name, analytic philosophy prioritises analysis. Speculative philosophy, on the other hand, uses analysis along with two other, equally important methods; synopsis ('viewing together') and synthesis. We can understand synopsis as the method of creating comparative overviews to point out inconsistencies. These overviews might pertain to domains usually considered separate (such as physical phenomena and social phenomena) or to theories from disciplines usually considered separate. They give an important place to detailing the historical development of conceptual approaches. The third method, synthesis, is unique to speculative philosophy. It involves providing concepts (or basic categories) to overcome inconsistences, in an endeavour that is as descriptive and imaginative as it is rigorous and systematic. The aim of these three methods is to develop understanding as a useful, lived experience of the world and human beings, rather than to arrive at timeless, objective truths.

Basic assumptions as foundational metaphors

Lakoff and Johnson's theory of metaphor, including its development over the past twenty-five years, offers an accessible way of understanding that our concepts both shape and are shaped by experience. They emerge in our everyday, embodied experience and are elaborated upon in specific cultures and communities. The two most important aspects of metaphorical concepts, in this regard, is that they are powerful organisers of our experience and that they can change. Uncovering how our entire conceptual system depends on metaphors, even prior to language, brings out the point that experience and understanding are not objective and unmediated, but that they are also not completely subjective. The meaning that emerges in both experience and understanding is related to genuine aspects of our bodies and a world that is actually there; it is the way we both have and contact a world, as human beings, cultures and individuals.

We can approach the idea of basic assumptions about the world in a similar way to metaphor. They would not make sense without relating to an actual world but at the same time they influence the way we experience the world. In *Metaphors We Live By* Lakoff and Johnson named these more foundational metaphors *ontological metaphors* and they include our propensity to understand many phenomena as entities and substances, or *physical things*. We do this with countless phenomena. Think of the weather, the internet, the future or a friendship, a connection, an illness. These are all phenomena that have no real entity structure, defined borders or material existence, but yet we often refer to them as though they do. Whether they are the result of living in a culture highly influenced by materialism or whether they simply make intangible phenomena more tangible—which could well be a result of the highly developed visual capacity of humans—is difficult to ascertain. Even so, they do show that basic assumptions reverberate strongly through our conceptual system and offer a justification for trying out alternatives when the prevailing assumptions hit their limits—as they clearly do in theories about feeling, or in the gap between the physical world and our experience.

Lakoff and Johnson's work, and the field of embodied

cognition generally, is highly influenced by pragmatism. This school of philosophy is centrally concerned with the practical consequences of our ideas and beliefs, including the effects on our experience. Pragmatism is particularly useful for reflecting on scientific inquiry and the kind of truth it leads to, which pragmatists see in terms of agreements among people and practical outcomes rather than objectivist accounts of truth. In *The Meaning of the Body*, Johnson develops the work of and draws inspiration from the American pragmatist philosopher John Dewey. In doing so he invokes the principle of continuity, which states that the same principles can explain both physical and mental phenomena; they are not different *kinds* of thing, but are both natural phenomena, making the human mind both evolutionarily and developmentally continuous with nature. This is a metaphysical principle of the ilk of speculative philosophy. Indeed, through their work Lakoff and Johnson have consistently put forward the same tenet as is being attempted here (and has countless times in the history of philosophy) of moving beyond absolute distinctions between subject and object. One way that Johnson sums up the problem and proposes a move forward is worth quoting at length:

> If we could only disabuse ourselves of the mistaken idea that thought must somehow be a type of activity *ontologically* different from our other bodily engagements (such as seeing, hearing, holding things and walking) then our entire understanding of the so-called mind/ body problem would be transformed. We would cease to interpret the problem as to how two completely different kinds of things (body and mind) can be united in interaction. Instead, we would rephrase the problem as that of explaining how increasing levels of complexity within organisms can eventually result in the emergence of progressively more reflective and abstractive cognitive activities, activities we associate with "mind".[2]

This paragraph sums up much of what has been pointed out already. It mentions that a new way of approaching the mind/body problem centres on explanations of emergence and levels of complexity, something that all the authors so far discussed make reference to. They do this either explicitly (talking about hierarchies of functioning in brain, body and interaction patterns) or implicitly (using the language of dynamic, complex systems). This points to a strong, identifiable change emerging in many branches of science, not least biology and neuroscience. But here in Johnson's remarks we can also see that the shift in thinking is towards an *ontology* of *activity*. This means that a better way to characterise *what exists* is as activity, rather than as the physical matter of materialism. We are not claiming that physical matter doesn't exist or isn't important, but rather, that we should develop theories and language that understand physical matter and objects as emerging from activity. To state this even more clearly, we should understand physical matter and objects as kinds of activity.

The reference to John Dewey's philosophy by Johnson provides an interesting juncture. Dewey is known as a prominent pragmatist philosopher, but he is also seen by some as an important figure in a branch of speculative philosophy sometimes termed *process philosophy*. Process philosophy is not a straightforward tradition to define. Many philosophers have not identified with the name but have nonetheless used a process approach or developed a process metaphysics. This is applicable to many philosophers and all the way back to the Ancient Greeks. For example Heraclitus (c. 535-475 BCE) is considered a process philosopher. It also includes philosophers who are currently being taken up in some areas of biology, such as Charles Sanders Peirce (1839-1914). But before discussing the tradition and which terminology might best suit our contemporary situation we should first outline a process approach and how it begins to provide a solution to the problem of dualism.

Process philosophy

Even the term *process* makes a link to one of the two phrases Jonas uses to describe the synthesis that is necessary to overcome dualism; that the opposites be seen as *phases of becoming*. A more tangible way to express this is simply that we should conceive of both the physical and mental (or the body and conscious experience) as processes. This means that rather than seeing human consciousness and feeling as emerging from and dependent upon the physical, both consciousness and the body should be understood as emerging from and dependent upon processes. We could just as easily use Johnson's term *activity* here; they mean the same thing. One of the major shifts in this way of seeing the world is from understanding phenomena as *objects in space* to understanding them as *processes in time*. Of course it can be difficult to suddenly make this shift because we are so used to projecting entity structure and experiences of the body in space onto phenomena.

Nicholas Rescher provides an accessible overview of the themes of process philosophy in his book *Process Metaphysics*. Such an introduction is welcome in the tradition because schemas in process metaphysics can be notoriously complex and difficult to grasp. Importantly, Rescher says of process philosophy:

> However greatly positions differ in other regards
> (and they do so enormously), they all agree in
> seeing time, process, change and historicity as
> among the fundamental categories for
> understanding the real.[3]

He tables the following comparisons with the more familiar substance philosophy:[4]

Substance Philosophy	Process Philosophy
discrete individuality	interactive relatedness
separateness	wholeness (totality)
condition (fixity of nature)	activity (self-development)
uniformity of nature	innovation / novelty
unity of being (individualised specificity)	unity of law (functional typology)
descriptive fixity	productive energy, drive etc
classificatory stability	fluidity and evanescence
passivity (being acted upon)	activity (agency)

Even if we do not immediately understand every phrase in this comparison we can see how strong the themes of change and activity are, which in itself reminds us of the tendencies coming through in all the fields already discussed. But even if they are quite clear, these comparisons are also a little misleading. They tempt us to simply replace substance concepts with process concepts. However the conceptual change is more than a switch in conceptual content, which can seem like another switch to an opposite. Rather, the change is also one of conceptual style. It involves a different way of understanding.

One of the most important features of process philosophy is that it resists totalising knowledge. It never sees itself as complete but as always adjusting in relation to a changing world, finding the best ways of making the world intelligible. Thus, the philosophy itself should be in process. We cannot stand outside of the world and our particular viewpoints, but we can find more or less accurate and useful means of understanding it. These will naturally change as the world changes. However, this need not mean that the fundamental themes or categories of process philosophy are in some sort of constant flux, which could lead to similar problems to those of post-modernism. It only means that even the most apparently fixed or stable phenomena, such as the laws of nature described in science, are *in principle* subject to change even if that is over extremely long periods of time. Thus, Rescher says "On this perspective, the world's only pervasive permanence is change itself."[5]

Change as a basic category

One of the most interesting implications of positing change as a basic category (or the fundamental assumption we choose to make about the world) is that it entirely alters our perspective on causation. Change is simply always, already happening. Our task is to discover the principles by which we can identify change, the ways things tend to happen. It is very difficult to get beyond the idea that we should identify substances or objects and *then* the forces acting on them or, in the case of life, animating them. Saying that there is nothing *beneath* or *before* change is the same as saying that *change is cause of itself*. Here we could just as easily use the terms activity or movement. Change and cause are, at a fundamental level, the same. Processes are kinds of change. They exist and they either continue or change. Of course we can still identify particular causes, as kinds of change. But even when we identify causes that are very stable and consistent, such as laws of nature, we are still in an important sense placing a boundary around the relations between phenomena, in the way that everything we observe is already in a situation and we observe that situation. For example, what was it that made me wake up this morning? We could say it was because I'd had enough sleep after going to bed early. Or we could also explain it in terms of variations in my body's hormones and neurotransmitters, which create a circadian rhythm and influence my body temperature. But one night of sleep also depends upon the particular rhythms developed in my body over my lifetime of sleeping and waking, which in turn depends upon the evolution of sleep-wake cycles in humans. This cycle is repeated, within a range, in each individual person and occurs in relation to the movements of the earth around the sun. But another cause of my body existing in the first place was conception so that required certain circumstances in my parents' lives to occur which depended upon numerous other preconditions—and so on ad infinitum. In a completely real sense, albeit one that is difficult to grasp, all processes just are forms of change that occur in relation to each other.

The idea of change as a basic assumption doesn't come from nowhere. It is the single factor that we can observe in all phenomena, physical and non-physical. However, because this is speculative philosophy, change is nonetheless the assumption of a category. This means that we are saying that change *exists* while knowing that we cannot *ultimately* explain this in its entirety. It is fair to say then, that the whole of change is unfathomable; it is beyond our intellectual grasp, not like another realm but as a limit placed by our humanness. We are part of it and we cannot ultimately get an outside perspective on the whole. This might seem unhelpful to some. Why say that the most basic fact of existence is unknowable as a whole? Firstly, doing so explicitly acknowledges something that all theories about the world do anyway. They choose an unprovable starting point. Secondly, change as a basic category will make much more sense of life. This will help to restore life as central to the world rather than an anomaly. Already we can say that life is change within certain limits for a particular period of time, a certain kind of process, emerging from the activity that already is the world. And already this seems more sensible than trying to figure out what animates essentially dead matter. Finally, accepting that we cannot know the whole of change at once (or objectively) allows us to identify the most basic ways that we *can* perceive and understand change and this builds *perspective* into our theory.

Facing inwards and outwards

Jonas suggests understanding the natural duality we observe in the world—the most apparent of which is of experience and the physical world—as *phases of becoming* but also as *faces of its being*.[6] This is one way of describing how we can both identify change and preserve perspective; any process faces both inwards and outwards. We might describe the inward facing perspective and the outward facing perspective but we cannot describe or understand them simultaneously. We tend to switch between the two. One way to think about this is to reflect on the difference between *a process* and simply *process*. When we refer to *a process* we are placing a boundary, demarcating an activity. We can define the activity as what it is itself or we can define it by how the situation around it makes it possible, but if we try to do both we are back to the whole of change—or *process* as distinct from *a process*. Not only that, defining the activity depends on my being able to differentiate it. It depends not only on what exists but on my being able to notice it.

This brings up one of the most difficult but potentially fruitful aspects of a process approach, that *differentiation* refers to both the way things happen and the way we notice phenomena by drawing a distinction. This is an inherent but useful paradox. To explain differentiation, we need to try to understand how processes come into existence. We can say that processes emerge by differentiating from the wholeness of change. Importantly we shouldn't think of change as *another realm* but, to recap, as more like a wholeness of movement or activity—perhaps as a flux or just as *happening*. For a distinguishable process to emerge from this change or happening there must be some kind of separation but that separation (or differentiation) must be in relation to all that exists, both causally and in its inherent self-activity. One way to think about this is to understand differentiation as a *dialectic*;

this is a more dynamic mode of expressing duality. Like duality, dialectic is based on a *twoness*, but also includes the wholeness of the reality so that the two sides imply one another. They are not so much a spectrum from one opposite end to another as two perspectives on differentiation, one facing outwards and one facing inwards. So while we cannot grasp the entirety of change, we can characterise existence at its most basic level in terms of two dialectics: process/relation and inner aspect/outer aspect.

Of course, these are very abstract notions but they are important for being clear about the basic ways we understand the world and for ways we can later understand causes, as well as where the limits are for understanding causes. They will also make more sense in the later discussion of living systems. For now, we can think of it in relation to the mind-body problem, even though this explanation will need elaboration later. So, although it is a somewhat rudimentary statement at this point, we can think of the self as a process, with experience the inner aspect of that process and the body as an outer aspect of that process. Experience is simply the process from the inside and the physical body the process as encountered from the outside. The difference from the more ordinary dualism of mind and body is that the mind and body are not different kinds of thing at all. They are different perspectives on the one process. There is no absolute break here. There is an apparent separation, but one that I believe is quite faithful to experience. While we can look at any process as always occurring in relation to all that exists, or as a position in existence, the only process that we are inside is our own. We can identify other processes or engage in broader processes but we are not fully *inside* them. Aside from our own experience, we encounter all other processes from the outside and this is in itself a relation. This doesn't mean that we somehow directly contact the world through our experience, but it does suggest that we *contact* change in a different way than we do by *observing* other processes, which is necessarily from the outside. Importantly, this doesn't privilege one perspective over the other. One is not more real or more direct or superior. They together make up what we can know of what exists.

The concept of the dialectic has featured strongly in the development of speculative philosophy, particularly through the nineteenth century.[7] For our purposes here, however, it can be kept quite simple, as a way of invoking the principle that all processes occur in relation to each other, in relation to the whole, and that *perspective taking* is a fundamental feature of the emergence of new processes. The dynamic aspect of a new process is also, from the outer aspect, a perspective-in-relation. As an abstract principle, this in itself is difficult to grasp but should become clearer in its application. Importantly, the notion of dialectic helps us to reflect on the discussion of enactivism. Enactivism prioritises dynamic action in its account of embodied cognition, so it fits very well with a metaphysics (or basic category) of change. However one of the problems identified with the focus on dynamic activity is that we can lose sight of the structuring of activity and interaction, including experience. The idea of a dialectic of process/relation being the most fundamental way that we can understand the world, as distinct from the whole of change which we cannot grasp, identifies processes, separating them from relations so that we may characterise them. But, perhaps more importantly, it makes space for an explanation for why being conscious feels separate from other processes that we observe. It is the inner perspective or aspect of what is, from the outer aspect, an entirely relational self. This important relationship of our conscious experience with all that we find around ourselves is the most direct example and accessible way of understanding that process/relation is an inward/outward relationship rather than a relationship of opposites.

Another way to think about this is through a similar paradox that arises when we attempt to think about change. To think about or characterise any thing or process we must identify a stable aspect of that thing or process. Thus, our knowing change actually relies on repetition, which is another way of saying structure. Structure simply refers to that which stays the same during processes of change. A more tangible way to state this is in terms of Peirce's insight, often mentioned in embodied cognitive science and some fields of contemporary biology, that nature has the tendency to take habits. In an important way, repetition also points to change in its sense of movement or activity because it highlights continuity as active—as a *keeping on going* that is as relevant to change as *becoming different* is—particularly because becoming different relies on the perception of difference as much as its actuality. Furthermore, the *order* that repetition or structure refers to enables us to identify that which changes; its *disorder*. So, for example, order and disorder are meaningless on their own. We can only know one in relation to the background of the other. Thus, we can describe the forms that change takes as the interplay of order and disorder. Once again, these terms are useful not only for their content, but for the effect that they have on our way of conceptualising. They generate the sense that nothing is fixed or absolute, but they also contain a balance that encourages us forward without disintegrating into relativism. There is much that we can meaningfully state as a result of such concepts and the influence on our experience should show that to us. They should help us to bring new meaning forward.

But, to reiterate a point made about change, new meaning doesn't emerge from nowhere. It must be a change in perspective on what is already there, but this in itself changes what exists. To explain, some kind of stability or structuring surrounds or contains any process, thereby allowing it to change. This is what existing in relation means and, importantly, this points to the *inherent creativity* that is change. This point might be easier to understand by referring again to metaphor. Recall that metaphor highlights and hides aspects of the world and this applies not only to understanding but also to experience. So this explains how experience occurs in relation, but that it could also be different. If we use a different metaphor we might have a different experience but there are limits to the new metaphors we can use, and usually they arise naturally in our experience whether that be human, cultural or individual. For example, the metaphor that the body is a machine arose with some deliberateness. One way to say this is that it emerged as a powerful analogy in science that did help to solve, or at least simplify, certain problems and eventually worked its way into the broader culture as a metaphor. Interestingly, we can see this as bringing forward some kind of reality. It is useful in certain contexts to focus on the mechanistic, one-way relations of processes in the body, such as seeing the heart as a pump. But it remains difficult to contact anything unless it is through this relatedness. We can't really say whether the structure or relation exists until we differentiate it. So while the dialectic of process/relation understands the two aspects as equally real, they can *also* be seen as a relation of actual/potential. We can make this more comprehensible by saying that change, as a whole, is as much *potentiality* as actuality. Again, these are very difficult concepts to understand in the abstract. We can try restating it as reality folds inward and unfolds simultaneously, but the unfolding cannot be known in its entirety, only by the relations that we pick out.

Of course, and perhaps unfortunately, this is a cursory introduction to the concerns of speculative philosophy. Many philosophers spend whole careers outlining and debating the details of metaphysical approaches. The idea here, however, is different. It is to demonstrate the need for shifts in thinking *like those*, even if this example is imperfect in its detail. At the same time, the fundamental shift towards change as a basic assumption and process/relation as the dialectic by which we know it should prove itself by supporting the discussion of feeling through this book. This aim is supported by speculative philosopher Andrew Reck's statement that

> Simplicity of theory, spelled out in a manageable
> list of categories, activates the creative imagination.
> The philosopher whose theory is simple is better
> able to keep before his mind the considerations
> relevant to his categories and their extrapolations.[8]

Speculative naturalism

The dualism of materialism and idealism has had a deep and lasting impact on the development of Western culture, one of which we do not have anywhere near enough collective awareness. Even though many of us have different personal perspectives on it—in terms of personal beliefs about the physical world, the role, if any, of higher powers and even death—we can no doubt all identify ways in which this dualism underpins all kinds of actions and attitudes towards each other and the world. There is very good reason, then, to offer new ways of conceptualising basic assumptions that can be grasped by more people than just philosophers, so that philosophy can help to guide change in difficult times.

The concepts offered here are an example of a process metaphysics. However, the way we locate them within a tradition is important for its broader ramifications. While it could suffice, *process philosophy* turns out not to be the best term for this tradition. In academia, process philosophy is not always identified with a tradition. Indeed the name is very often identified with the work of a single philosopher, Alfred North Whitehead (1861-1947) whose seminal work *Process and Reality* was published in 1929. Another complicating factor is that many process philosophers identifying as such are process theologians, understanding God or divinity through process approaches.[9] So while these philosophers are also deeply concerned with process approaches to nature and the world, the context is different from what is being attempted here.

Arran Gare describes the tradition that process metaphysics belongs to—along with other philosophies such as Peircean semiotics and naturalized phenomenology—as *speculative naturalism*. The basic tenet of *naturalism* is that the cosmos should be explained without appeal to supernatural forces or spiritual entities. For naturalism they do not exist and we can locate all phenomena and their explanation within nature. However, naturalism has also been, particularly through the twentieth century, closely associated with materialism and analytic philosophy, both of which take the possibility of an objective viewpoint on the physical world as given. Through a detailed discussion of the development of analytic philosophy and its problems, Gare essentially recovers the term. He defines speculative naturalism as theories that are centrally concerned with how nature evolved such that human consciousness emerged, in human beings that are both part of and able to reflect on the natural world, including with the creation of science. This appears to be exactly the kind of naturalism that Gallagher suggests is the next step for a theory of embodied cognition:

> If enactivism is a form of naturalism, it does not
> endorse the mechanistic definition of nature often
> presupposed by science, but contends that nature
> cannot be understood apart from the cognitive
> capacity that we have to investigate it.[10]

Gare locates the tradition of speculative naturalism as beginning with Friedrich Schelling (1775-1854) and continuing to the present day. An important aspect of this tradition is that it acknowledges the problems of materialism and idealism, and goes beyond them by making consciousness a central concern while also seeing nature as the starting point for investigation, because consciousness is a natural phenomenon. This explains why some of the most creative work currently emerging in the tradition is in the fields of philosophical and theoretical biology. Such creative work has been particularly influenced by variations of process metaphysics developed in the early twentieth century, which Gare describes as "expressions of a renaissance"[11] in speculative naturalism that is currently being revived in science after being marginalised by analytic philosophy.

However, science is in no way privileged. In fact speculative naturalism is described as continuing the humanistic traditions of the Renaissance, which essentially led to the *Radical Enlightenment*.[12] This enlightenment is distinguished from the *Moderate Enlightenment*, which led to the dominant position of mechanistic, reductionist science and its corollaries in all areas of human affairs, including economics and politics.[13]

Thus, speculative naturalism should be seen as a part of the Radical Enlightenment, as a strong tradition in the humanities and sciences that never disregarded life but in fact centralised it. The theoretical rumblings of the past twenty-five years, already mentioned in relation to theories of cognition and feeling, are part of a much longer, distinguished tradition. These rumblings are certainly getting stronger, but they have also been there all along.

6

Developing processes and ordering relations

IN CASE WE SEEM TO HAVE VEERED too far away from theories of feeling and emotion, now is a good time to take stock and to reemphasise the importance of the speculative categories, or new metaphors. The reasons for the form of Part One of this book have also hopefully become apparent. These chapters attempted to provide a thorough but accessible critical overview of some of the main theories that currently influence our understanding of feeling and emotion, from experimental psychology, philosophy and neuroscience. To this end, those chapters are examples of the methods of analysis and synopsis. The purpose of the level of detail provided was to reveal problems and inconsistencies but also similar themes emerging in these overlapping fields, as well as to explain concepts that are important for later theory. All of the theorists referred to report extensive empirical research; that is not what is in question here. Rather, I intended to demonstrate the need for a deeper conceptual shift that is *already implied* in the interpretations of research, using the tools of speculative philosophy. These tools take the form here of the process/relation and inner aspect/outer aspect schema suggested. I offer this schema as a basis for synthesis. Its application should build theory that can reconcile problems. In keeping with the tradition of speculative naturalism this schema should also, very generally, support constructive reflection on theories of the emergence of consciousness from nature. Such reflection should in turn provide a better understanding of feeling and emotion.

Even before further discussion, the basic principle that change is knowable only as inner aspect/outer aspect supports a rethinking of one of the major problems identified in Barrett's work but pertaining to neuroscience more generally; that of hallucination. Very simply, the idea that, unbeknown to us, we live in virtual worlds generated by the hypotheses of our brains degrades human experience. It is seen as *nothing more* than brain states. Even if described as complex, these brain states—the physical firing of neurons or complex networks of neurons—are considered real and our experience is somehow *less real*. Rather than convincing us of the truth of materialism, this view of experience should alert us to what must be a fundamental error, because it goes against our fundamental, everyday experience as beings in the world; that we exist and are having an experience. This doesn't mean that we are never mistaken about our perceptions or experiences but that generally we can be fairly sure that our experience is happening in a world that is also happening. That we know, or *are*, it as an inner aspect posits that experience is equally real to any physical or physiological process, but differently encountered and known.

Admittedly, much more discussion is needed to show the worth of this schema, particularly for understanding feeling. For now it is important to point out that the idea that any process has an inner aspect does not imply that all processes have some kind of consciousness. It means that *in principle* we can imagine a perspective or position from the inside. This applies to both living and non-living processes. Even so, because consciousness has emerged from natural processes, at some stage in evolution the inner aspect becomes something like our human consciousness. Thus, we need to understand the processes that could possibly give rise to an inner aspect such as ours, such that experience is possible and actually happens. If we want to use a basic ontology of processes, which says that processes are the most fundamental way to characterise what exists, one way to frame this inquiry is in terms of the emergence of a human self. We need to understand this emergence in terms of both development and individuation in a life span, and within the longer process of evolution.

Of course, this is a very big story to tell, one that many people in many disciplines are working on. For the purposes of this book, and a deeper understanding of feeling, some concepts from theoretical biology are key for a process theory of the emergence of a self, particularly to help us reflect on the nature of causes. Two concepts that are central to the entire discussion are emergence and hierarchical organisation.

Emergence

Emergence is a causal concept. It describes a situation in which a phenomenon comes into existence that cannot be described only in terms of its constituents. A simpler way to say this is that the whole is more than the sum of its parts, or in this case, processes. The concept of autocatalysis (in chemistry) is an example of emergence. Autocatalysis "refers to situations in which the chemical reactants that take part in a system accelerate the processes by which they themselves are produced."[1] This can lead to threshold effects where previously random chemical reactions suddenly become ordered in a network of reactions. This new order that arises can become stable and self-sustaining. In this case there are no new constituents or parts in the system but the new *level of order* that arises is a genuinely new phenomenon. This new stable level can in turn become the constituent for another new phenomenon or level to emerge, and so on.

For a very different but equally valid example we can apply this description to cognition and learning, as was briefly mentioned in relation to the development of the container schema in the discussion of metaphor. In the process of learning, which in children is often highly motivated exploration and discovery, repetitive activities eventually simply give rise to understanding. The threshold that is reached is a new kind of order, an emergent phenomenon, and we can say this regardless of whether it is accompanied by a change in physiology. However, when some situation as this—say, the emergence of a new understanding—is taken as an isolated example, emergence as a causal principle can appear to have a quality of *just happening* and then be seen as not providing any real explanation. In some senses this is fair to say, as emergence is a causal description without an external agent. There is no *acting upon*; the reconfiguration of a process is from within, albeit always in relation to a context. However, the *just happening* is better seen as standing in for the fact that any causal explanation can only ultimately end at the whole of change. Despite this limitation, and well before that endpoint, we can find excellent ways to describe how stabilities are created and persist, in both development and evolution, such that novelty then becomes possible. For instance, while the emergence of understanding of some particular aspect of the world in a child is a moment of genuine novelty for that child, it rests on all the stable processes that created not only that particular little one but human beings, their bodies and brains and potential for experience in the first place. This in turn is based on the fundamental necessity of stable relations with an actual world all through the evolutionary process.

Causes extend out potentially indefinitely yet within stable frameworks of processes that we can identify and describe. One way to theorise these frameworks is as levels in hierarchical organisation, with emergence an important causal concept. Emergence occurs between levels in the sense that phenomena can be characterised as emerging from constituents (lower level) within environmental constraints (upper level) such that causation is both downwards and upwards in the hierarchy. Both the level immediately below and that immediately above have a causal relationship to the emergent level, which is nonetheless novel in its separateness. It cannot be fully explained by either reducing it to the constituents or equalling it to surrounding phenomena. The swarm behaviour of bees, for instance, relies on the existence of individual bees and certain environmental situations but the behaviour of the whole cannot be described in terms of the individual bees themselves or seen as directly caused by the environment, even though it would not take place without either of these levels.

Identifying phenomena through the perspective of levels in a causal hierarchy is necessarily a *choice* and an *abstraction* from the world, which really is, even in a scientific sense, always a situation of complexity. Even so, the definition of a level is not wholly arbitrary. There must be some reliability in the process (something actual) otherwise we could not know anything. To continue our example, swarms appear again and again, even though they are not predictable. Despite our experience of them as obviously different from the bees themselves, our relation to the phenomenon (our ability to observe it) is stable. Describing levels and their causal relations genuinely makes sense of some situation of our choosing and allows us to discover causal relations but is also dependent upon our observations and definitions of what count as phenomena in the first place or what we are interested in understanding.[2]

While understanding causes in this way might appear to contradict experimentation in science, which aims to isolate phenomena to investigate them, it actually clarifies the point that experimental and empirical research (with its varieties of methods, tools and definitions) is in itself a set of constraints, a causal environment. Whatever causal sequences or relations are discovered there may or may not translate directly back into the world or the problem we are trying to solve. For example, new pharmaceutical drugs often have unforseen side effects (which are just effects) in some people but not others. Or a person's response to an emotional stimulus in an experimental setting may be quite unlike their response to a similar stimulus in a natural life setting. In ecology, a species introduced to control one problem might overpopulate and create new problems. In chemistry, a one-to-one chemical reaction might happen in a petri dish but not in a plant. In physics, activity observed with specialized equipment at the quantum level may or may not scale up in any meaningful way to phenomena that we normally perceive. Nature is sometimes predictable and sometimes not, but always complex.

Complexity and change

Concepts of emergence and hierarchies are a way of getting a handle on complexity. In their book *Hierarchy Theory: A Vision, Vocabulary and Epistemology,* biologists Timothy Allen and Valerie Ahl discuss the way that both definitions and dynamics are central to hierarchy theory. Their definition of complexity reinforces the discussion of levels:

> We defined a complex system as one in which fine
> details are linked to large outcomes. In order to
> describe adequately a complex system, several
> levels need to be addressed simultaneously.[3]

In *Development and Evolution: Complexity and Change in Biology,* Stanley Salthe offers a different but complementary definition with a stronger focus on actual dynamics:

> A situation is complex when two or more systems
> occupy the same physical coordinates but do not
> regularly interact.[4]

Both definitions involve levels of scale. Rather than the physical parts of mechanism, which does not grapple well with situations of complexity, hierarchy theory tends to focus on frequencies of interaction. This refers to separation in time rather than in space. Often, lower levels in a hierarchy exhibit faster rates of interaction than higher levels. For example, unless we have specialist knowledge of the human body and particularly physiology (and perhaps even if we do have this knowledge) we are likely to identify separation in the body such as organs and systems in terms of spaces. If we shift the focus to processes we become more interested in the different time scales in the body. Both chemical and neural processes exhibit concentration and network effects that emerge from the lower level, faster dynamics of individual cells and neurons. Rates such as heart rate and breathing will act as environmental constraints on many lower level faster cellular processes because they change the rate of interactions across cell membranes. The events and conditions outside the body will influence the rates of processes within the body. Importantly, with all of these levels the causal influence flows both ways.

Hierarchies that are characterised in terms of levels of scale are probably easiest to understand in a situation of nestedness. For instance the human body is constituted of cells within organs within systems within the whole body. Salthe terms this the scalar hierarchy: "Entities in the scalar hierarchy are... wholes with nested parts extending downward in scale indefinitely".[5] We also need to keep in mind that while a human being, or any organism, seems a natural choice as an entity in nature, we could just as well choose a different scale. For example, if we are interested in population dynamics, then an individual human being will be a constituent of the level we are investigating (population) and larger scale environmental changes over longer periods of time will count as the most relevant environmental causes or constraints. Thus, scalar hierarchies also extend upwards indefinitely. Non-nested hierarchies also exist, such as food chains in ecology, but such hierarchies also need not be ecological or biological. For instance Allen and Ahl give the example of the American legal system in which the Supreme Court and the Constitution constrain the behaviour of state courts and individual police officers.[6] While this appears a more abstract hierarchy, it is interesting that we can see even here that the activity of officers on the ground, so to speak, will be quicker but more generalised than activity in the courts. This refers not to the activity of the people involved but to the activity of identifying and dealing with an infraction at various levels. The infraction becomes different because it is defined differently at different levels and usually the higher up the hierarchy, the slower the process of dealing with it.

Initially, it can be difficult to grasp different forms of hierarchy. Salthe, and Allen and Ahl name different kinds, which focus more on either definitions and types (such as evolutionary types) or dynamics and stages (such as developmental stages). Rather than going into the detail of different kinds of hierarchies and how they relate with each other (which can be confusing) we can explore the example of me now as a living self. The most straightforward hierarchy to interpret is me as a scalar hierarchy in this moment. Right now, various levels of physiological process are taking place within my body as a whole. A multitude of processes are going on at the cellular level coordinated by various neural and chemical signals from which emerge higher level coordinating processes and eventually my whole living body. This is all occurring within, and causally constrained by, the processes going on around me; changes in light, temperature, food availability, season and so on. Importantly, we should also include relationships and interactions with other people here, which greatly influence the lower level processes in my body as well as my body as a whole. We can see interaction, along with all the actions I take to alter my situation—such as seeking food and eating, settling down for sleeping, creating warmth with clothing—as activity in the same sense as physiology but at the level of the whole body. Seeing it this way can clarify the inner aspect/outer aspect relation. An outer aspect of these activities is behaviour and the inner aspect is experience, but we only know this at the level of the whole body. All the lower level processes, including brain patterns, are processes we can only know from the outer aspect. Saying that we can imagine them from the inner aspect simply means that we can theoretically separate them from other processes as having some kind of phenomenal integrity but we can only actually observe them from the outside. Separating out brain patterns also helps us to reflect on the definitional aspect of hierarchies. We can certainly observe brain patterns (to a degree) and discover their constituent lower level neuronal and synaptic processes and their environment either inside or outside of the body but defining them as a level must be at least *partly* an abstraction because they *never* exist separately from either a whole living body or a life history. This interpretation both resonates with and theoretically supports Damasio's discussion of the ways systems within the body, including various nervous systems, are relatively distinct but *at the same time* functionally blended. This "integrated mutuality"[7] gives rise to a whole, functioning body as well as to our human experience.

Interestingly, in the field of enactivism, Gallagher builds on work by Francisco Varela, who argues that "cognition involves processes on... three timescales". Gallagher terms these timescales the elementary, integrative and narrative:

1. The *elementary* scale (between 10 and 100 milliseconds)
2. The *integrative* scale (varying from 0.5 to 3 seconds)
3. The *narrative* scale (above 3 seconds)[8]

He says "The elementary scale is the basic timescale of neurophysiology. It corresponds to the intrinsic cellular rhythms of neuronal discharges."[9] These processes become integrated at the second timescale, which neurophysiologically "involves the integration of cell assemblies".[10] The key point for the integrative timescale is that it phenomenologically "corresponds to the experienced living present, the level of fully constituted cognitive operation".[11] Gallagher's discussion here demonstrates the use of the hierarchical three-levels perspective and how it can be applied to separate the level of experience from underlying neural processes. However it is also, clearly, an abstraction because this particular hierarchy must rely on a whole, living body. These points support my earlier claim that Damasio's recent work provides an excellent counterpart to the enactivist perspective, *if placed within this broader set of ideas*, including hierarchy, emergence *and* the fundamental process metaphysics.

Another important description of me as a living self is in terms of my particular stage of development. Salthe defines development as "predicitable, irreversible change"—something that resonates all too well with my current stage of development, which happens to be middle-age. My whole body system is at a particular stage, within the range of what is possible for humans at this age, having already moved through certain identifiable stages. While change is most obvious in the early stages of embryonic and foetal development, followed by early life and childhood, my system will continue to exhibit certain stages characteristic of human beings. It may also exhibit stages that are more generalizable to mammals or vertebrates, because I can also be defined within a hierarchy of evolutionary stages.

While these examples show us something about hierarchies, they might also convey something of how difficult it is to characterise change in complex situations. At best we need more than one explanation. The hierarchies that we pick out can often seem more like a static snapshot of a situation than a full account of changing dynamics. We cannot both focus in on one level and keep in mind the dynamics of another level. We can only see how other levels relate to the level we are observing. This no doubt influences the temptation to make lower level brain states—in the sense of lower than the whole body or experience—the only explanatory level. Another way to say this is with the concepts of analog (continuous) and digital (discrete). We think of change as dynamic and in this sense continuous, but often we only notice it as discrete. For instance a parent will suddenly notice a developmental milestone in her toddler. We often characterise development in this way, as sudden jumps; a digital mode. Yet, as Salthe mentions "the material situation is fuzzy–or really analog".[12] In some sense, however, this might depend on our vantage point. A behaviour might appear for the first time as though reorganisation and the emergence of a new level of order has happened quite suddenly (digital) but the lower level processes for this (say, brain and body changes) may have been gradual and afforded by the higher level environment in a gradual, or analog, way.

For the moment we should keep in mind that change can occur in two ways—continuous and smooth transitions or sudden jumps—but that the appearance of change as either of these depends also on the position of the observer. This is not in the sense of the observer directly influencing the process observed, but with regard to distance in scale, which can be either temporal or spatial. For example sudden jumps appear continuous in a bigger time scale or from further away, or when we focus in on a continuous process, we might find that its constituent processes appear discrete. Thus we can start to notice a familiar theme emerging here as in our understanding of embodied cognition; the theme of dynamic and structure. Allen and Ahl's statement reminds of this:

> While our experiences of the world are linked to
> change over time (dynamics), our definitions,
> which correlate with patterns of repeating
> experiences, are static and available to serve as
> elements in cognitive models.[13]

We need to keep this natural duality in mind. In fact the issues in hierarchy theory are not just about the need for more than one description but about the *relation between* the two descriptions, or the relation between dynamic and structure.[14] While this relation is ultimately, within the schema of metaphysics presented, unknowable as a whole, we can approach dynamic and structure as important perspectives on causation. Dynamic interactions are more readily associated with efficient causation, which simply means processes in which we can identify the transfer of energy. Relations, on the other hand, are more readily identified with final causation—the tendencies towards end states, particularly those that are built in by the evolutionary process. This second type of causation is currently unpopular in biology, possibly even ridiculed more broadly. Final causation will be further discussed later.

Consideration of the principles of emergence and levels in hierarchical organization also has an effect on our way of thinking, in the way of the paradox named earlier. More than one description is necessary for an account of any phenomenon. While, according to the schema presented in this book, the most basic and paradigmatic positions are from the inside and from the outside, it is helpful to imagine a switching between modes as zooming in to observe process and zooming out to observe relations. This helps to describe the way that any process exists for itself but also as a relation to its immediately surrounding levels along with, eventually, to all other processes. Another way of explaining this is to conceptualise a level as a process in itself but also as a mediating layer between other processes. An example based on the timescales mentioned earlier is that our integrated experience as it arises moment-to-moment is an emergent process in itself, but it also mediates the lower level neural processes and the broader environment of what is happening around us and what we are trying to do.

Surfaces and borders

Theoretically, all levels act as borders between other processes but some borders are stronger and more obvious in nature because they separate many lower level processes from a broader environment. Allen and Ahl describe these borders as natural surfaces:

> A natural surface is one that appears to remain in the same place, even when one changes from observing one type of signal to observing another. Since the filter at the surface works on a large number of signal types, the surface appears in the same place when observed under different criteria.[15]

One example of a natural surface is the membrane around an individual cell. Surfaces such as a cell membrane act as a relation between processes inside and outside the cell. While this includes the literal physical separation in space, the more important relational aspect of cell membranes is that they separate processes by filtering many types of information. Within the human body, for example, many different receptors can come into contact with the membrane of a given cell, setting off various complex interactions within the cell. However the membrane is not a static filter like a sieve; molecules in the membrane itself change as a way of conveying information. The membrane is an active border, a process in itself.

When Allen and Ahl use the term natural here, they mean coinciding rather than necessarily part of nature the way we normally think of it. Borders constructed by people can also form natural entities. They offer the example of a national border. This example illustrates that while the border is a literal place that we can visit or point out on a map, many interactions across a border are regulated by information that isn't literally located at the border, such as laws about the movement of people and goods. The meaning of say, a truckload of grain, at an actual border exists because of processes beyond the physicality of the truck, goods and driver, and the meaning influences what will actually occur across that border as much or more than the physical items themselves. At the same time, these actual physical presences, along with gates, guards, etc are also a locus of activity. As along the cell membrane where there are a multitude of interactions of different molecules (ligands) and receptors (proteins), which is the process of the membrane in itself, borders and particularly border towns will have high levels of activity relevant to the ongoing creation and maintenance of the national border. Pointing out these similarities among processes we would usually consider separate—perhaps as natural and cultural or at least of human construction—highlights that activity simply follows certain themes. Constructing an entity, either by humans or in the very long evolutionary process, will follow some of the same principles and parameters because that is how anything comes to exist. At the same time, while the borders of a nation state might be considered self-sustaining to a certain extent, they are not as robust as certain kinds of natural systems. Their change is more directly determined, at least some of the time, by the decisions and actions of people rather than emerging as a natural reordering at a certain level of complexity. To understand the kind of entity that an organism is, and eventually a human self, we need to understand organisms as self-sustaining entities or systems, and characteristics of their formation and change over time. Such an explanation will contextualise and clarify many of the points about hierarchies and emergence.

Dissipative structures

The reason for explaining some of these details about levels in a hierarchy and emergence, and now self-organising systems, is not because such concepts are new or not being used much in fields such as biology and ecology but for the opposite reason. They are now fairly commonplace but their underlying principles do not receive enough explanation outside of specialised fields.[16] When such discussion does occur it exposes the need to reconsider our most basic metaphysical concepts, the metaphors we very deeply (in the words of Lakoff and Johnson) *live by*. Such reconsideration is not at all about undermining science and its achievements. Rather, it is about acknowledging that where we are now depends on those achievements but that where we should go depends on *also* being courageous enough to face up to the limits of science.

The broad application of a process metaphysics to understanding life is a good place to start. As already stated: life is change within certain limits for a particular period of time, a certain kind of process emerging from the activity that already is the world. We can then ask what kind of a process generates and sustains a living self and how this process exists in relation to surrounding processes. Salthe's explanation of dissipative systems provides some key answers to these questions. We have already seen that change over time is difficult to describe with any single type of hierarchy. Even though the limits of observation remain, understanding dissipative systems can help us to conceptualise the human self as a process over time.

The concept of a self-sustaining system means that enough order is created for change to be to a great degree contained within the system during the period of its existence. Self-organisation, then, includes the concept of "change referring primarily to a system itself rather than to its scalar hierarchical connections with the rest of nature."[17] The system develops as order is generated through the emergence of new levels within the system. These new levels mediate the relationship between the system and its environment in a way that the whole can be maintained. Of course the system does remain causally connected with an environment, or levels outside; Salthe's use of the term semi-autonomy is more accurate than the term closure, which is sometimes used to describe self-sustaining systems, because the system as a whole is still very much related to and causally influenced by its environment. Importantly though, as was touched on earlier, order can only be created and observed in relation to a background of disorder, so the maintenance of a system over time also relies on a certain degree of disorder. The term dissipative structure encapsulates this. Salthe defines dissipative structures as "organizations that dissipate energy and also entropy".[18] The system dissipates different kinds of disorder during different stages of its existence.

Very generally, the play of order and disorder establishes the life cycle of a dissipative structure. We can think of it as an overall cycle of increasing order and then increasing disorder. An immature system realises many more of its potential states while a mature system will realise more detailed or defined states, but a smaller proportion of potential states. Put more simply, an immature system is more fluid but less defined while a mature system is more defined but also more rigid. Eventually this rigidity reaches a tipping point and the system begins to senesce, meaning that it is of high enough structural complexity that its tendency to change reduces. The life cycle as described this way is quite straightforward to imagine when we think of the difference between small children and the elderly. The behaviour of small children is both more disordered but much more generalised than adults. Development during this time is about establishing order so that the system may continue to exist. An elderly person, on the other hand, will exist as a highly developed self, including a sense of self based on experiences as well as the more mundane physical, mental and emotional habits developed over a lifetime of activities and interactions. However, the trade-off for this stage of development is the decreased ability to change, including the ability to respond to new situations in a novel way. Adults usually exhibit a mid-point somewhere in between these two extremes, although where exactly depends on how development has gone. For example serious trauma early in life might lead to protective behaviour (physical or mental rigidity) in many situations in adulthood. Here the trade-off for survival is a decrease in the range of potential. The basic idea of the dissipative system is that different kinds of disorder are dissipated during different stages. Young children build up and release much more physical energy than the elderly, partly because energy is not as highly channelled or organised (physical entropy) while the apparent rigidity of old age is a quite natural outcome of being an individual for a long time. The ability to respond in fresh ways is reduced (informational entropy) but because it cannot be released, it will naturally lead the system into decline.

Another way to think about the play of types of order and disorder through stages is as degree of distance, with distance in itself something of a paradox. Young children are more highly attuned to and influenced by their interactions with adults, in particular caregivers. Over time the level of dynamic interaction recedes. We can think of it as new levels of order shifting interaction more to relations rather than direct dynamic influences on the system. That a child will grow out of the need for physical comfort every time something difficult or painful happens is a direct example of this. As development occurs the system becomes more differentiated. The increase in physical distance that occurs in this process is offset, in a way, by a decrease in distance in the sense of being able to understand more about the world and thereby engage in more detailed interactions with other people. At the other end of the spectrum, old age, the paradox of becoming a highly individuated self means that eventually the distance becomes too great for the system to continue to adjust in a way that maintains enough equilibrium.

Emergence of a self

A *self* emerges as a system collects the effects of its own functioning; change refers inwards in a "collecting / cascading cycle".[19] This is the basis of becoming an individual, or individuation. As stated, we can pick out knowable stages that occur in all or most human beings (development) but this is only one description of the system, which is also an actual, dynamic activity that becomes an individual through the accumulation of historical information (which is another way of saying collecting the effects of its own functioning). We can speak of the whole process of development and individuation, then, as the *ontogenetic trajectory*, with ontogeny meaning that it occurs within an individual lifespan.[20] A self, then, simply is a process that both maintains itself within a range for survival while fulfilling an ontogenetic trajectory that is of a type (such as human) and, simultaneously, *always also a unique individual* because of the accumulation of change (historical information) up until whatever time the process ends. When we place the notion of change referring inwards within the context of the ontogenetic trajectory (development and individuation over time) the concept of homeostasis begins to seem very limited. The maintenance of a stable enough state physiologically occurs within broader processes of change through the life cycle, which has the evolutionary inner momentum of developing through partially predictable stages but whose individuation is much less determined. In relation to the ontogenetic trajectory, Salthe favours the term *homeorhesis* (drawn from the work of theoretical biologist C.H. Waddington) to describe the return of a system *to its trajectory* following a disturbance.[21]

Using these terms and within an overall understanding of semi-autonomous systems, then, the sense of self that is, or supports, experience is an emergent level of not only the whole body, but the whole of life experience. Even if many lower level

113

processes in the body must remain within a range and much of our functioning is geared towards this (homeostasis) the emergent level of experience of an actual life trajectory is no less real. This means that the purposes we pursue consciously have effects beyond simple life maintenance, even if they emerge from, because they are constituted by, processes below conscious awareness. Our purposes cannot be completely free from lower levels, so that we stay alive, but neither are they directly determined by these lower levels.

Even so, we can only really say this clearly by using the inner aspect/outer aspect schema, otherwise we have no way of relating experience and the physical and physiological body. Without this relation, the brain needs to somehow stand in for the self rather than being seen as a participant in many processes at many levels of functioning. *How* brain functioning is separate from, and thereby relates to, some of these physiological processes is a most interesting question to pursue, but it makes no sense to place agency within the brain or to reduce experience to neural processes alone.

These examples of human life are offered because they are not difficult to observe. However their theoretical context is in no way anthropocentric, or making nature fit our human experience. Salthe describes the *organism* as the "paradigmatic dissipative structure";[22] the stages and their characteristics are observable in all living organisms. Furthermore, the idea of dissipative structures makes important links to other natural phenomena. While they describe living systems well they are also applicable to some non-living systems, for instance some weather patterns such as hurricanes. According to Salthe, the continuity of dissipative systems through nature "forms an important mythic link between humans and other natural forms."[23] However, even if some non-living dissipative systems move through similar stages as living systems, the degree of autonomy of living systems seems unique. That there is enough closure in living systems for change to be largely contained, for new levels and relations to emerge completely within the system, is a defining feature. This means that while a system is developing in relation to an environment, it is also developing in relation to its own history. A self emerges as both of these relations develop. While all phenomena can be characterised as causally within various hierarchies within nature, only living systems exhibit this *opening inward* that must rely on a partially contained history—or really memory in the broadest sense of the term. For now we can say that the outer aspect (or relation) that is as fundamental to any phenomenon as the inner aspect (or process) occurs in two ways in a living organism. It may even be the defining feature of life, this *double relation*. We can now turn to a relatively new field in biology, biosemiotics, which offers many conceptual resources to further explain this.

7

Genes, cells, and signs

SYSTEMS THAT ARE ALIVE in the way that has been described (collecting the effects of their own functioning over time) develop into selves. To say this another way: a certain kind of inwardness develops in semi-autonomous systems, an inwardness that depends on a relation to a present environment but also on a relation to individual history. By definition then, even a single-celled organism develops into a rudimentary form of self and somewhere along the evolutionary line the developing inwardness is experienced as differentiated feeling. Our human consciousness emerges in a graded way through evolutionary types. Of course, then, we expect animals that are closer to humans in an evolutionary sense to have some kind of inner experience such as feeling. The possible nature and quality of this experience will be explored later. For now we need to understand more about the evolutionary process that gives rise to selves, to opening inwards.

Identifying the self

For a system to collect the effects of its own functioning, develop through stages and become an individual, requires the formation of a robust border. Such a border needs to contain a multitude of processes and allow for the emergence of more complex levels within the system. The most obvious of these borders in humans is the skin around the entire body, which acts as a literal, physical and psychological border at the level of our experience. However, as with the membrane around an individual cell, the creation and maintenance of this border relies not only on the actual physical skin or even the actual, dynamic processes forming the skin as a living border and process in itself. Rather, the ongoing creation of the border (of any border) relies on all the processes that generate the whole self. These processes are much better characterised as processes of *identifying* the self than literal, physical places in space, even if those physical places play an important role in self-identification. The immune system, for example, arises from processes of recognising cells as either self or not-self. Such processes are central to the maintenance of the integrity of the whole body and the border of a human self—a border that, for the immune system, is distributed throughout the body.

The ability of a system to recognise or identify itself is of fundamental importance to its development as a living system and as an individual. Jesper Hoffmeyer and Claus Emmeche put it this way:

> For a system to be living, it must create itself, i.e.
> it must contain the distinctions necessary for its
> own identification as a *system*. Self-reference is
> the fundament on which life evolves, the most
> basal requirement.[1]

In the language of the speculative schema: the opening inward that forms more and more differentiated selves, evolutionarily speaking, is both a dynamic activity and a relation *to itself*, as well as always in relation to a changing environment. A self forms both through dynamic activity and through the formation of this double relation. The corollary of these concepts—which are fundamental to understanding selves and eventually to understanding experience and feeling—is that because processes always occur in relation to other levels of process, they are always *interpretive*. To rephrase this: all processes are also relations in that they mediate other processes and *this mediation is a form of communication or interpretation*. Returning to our earlier example of experience mediating lower

117

level neural processes and environmental situations, experience is a dynamic process in itself—we feel it as this—but it is also an interpretation in relation to the processes constituting it and those surrounding it.

Biosemiotics

Biosemiotics is a field of theoretical biology that makes sense of such interactive, interpretive processes in the natural world by understanding them as sign processes. It explains the communication processes by which an organism emerges from and relates to its world. Biosemiotics is centrally concerned with the transfer of information, but not in the way that it is often understood in contemporary biology, which tends to view information as something that physically exists and can be moved around. In his book, *Biosemiotics,* Hoffmeyer describes this tendency as the "reification of information" and sees it as hindering theoretical developments in biology, particularly in this use of a *transport metaphor.* Rather, biosemiotics acknowledges that information, as such, cannot exist outside of a system of interpretation; it requires a *someone* for whom it signals something. Information arises when a *relation* exists between a something (a phenomenon) and a someone (a system), which creates a relation to a third position (an effect). We can restate this more simply by saying that information only exists for an observer for whom it is relevant. This moves the concept of information away from physical objects and towards processes and relations. For instance, an instruction manual doesn't literally *contain* information, but meaning arises when it is engaged with by someone who can understand it and who has a reason to. Perhaps we can say that an instruction manual, as an object, creates the *potential* for someone to create meaning but not more than this. This biosemiotic understanding of signs is based on a system developed by the philosopher Charles

Sanders Peirce. It sees sign processes as essentially *triadic*, or based on three-way causal relations. Hoffmeyer explains that interactive, interpretive processes not only permeate but are the basis of living systems:

> Biosemiosis, the never-ending stream of sign
> processes that regulate and coordinate the
> behaviour of living systems, depends on the special
> receptivity that evolutionary systems over time
> have developed towards selected features of their
> environment. Peirce considered "the tendency [of
> things] to take habits"... —or, in more modern
> parlance, *self-organization* (the tendency for ever
> new regularities to arise in natural systems)—as the
> most fundamental characteristic of nature. And
> living systems are examples par excellence of the
> tendency to *take notice*... to detect regularities in
> their surroundings that, if properly interpreted,
> might guide them to perform well.[2]

Living systems are attuned to certain characteristics of the world in particular ways. One of the foundational concepts within biosemiotics is that of *umwelt*, from the work of biologist Jakob von Uexküll (1864-1944). *Umwelt* describes the surrounding world of an organism, which is actively created through its own perceptual engagement and ability to make distinctions. Thus, it is not an objective world but a world created in relation. However, a creature's *umwelt* is not entirely relative or subjective either. An organism can only live within an *umwelt* formed by ongoing attunements to actual regularities, developed in its life and in the evolutionary process, otherwise it would not survive. Hoffmeyer describes the way that repetition in nature is the basis of not simply phenomena in themselves, but phenomena as signs. All phenomena mean something to other living organisms. This is the basis of the view of the living world as a *semiosphere*.

119

Among biochemists, there is a rule of thumb saying that whenever nature keeps a store of energy (eg. food) there will also always be a species that makes a living on consuming it. I shall suggest a similar rule of thumb by saying that there never occurs a regularity or a habit in nature that has not *become a sign* for some other organism or species.[3]

If we can really grasp the point that all phenomena will also be a sign *of* something *for* one or two or a multitude of species, and that a single phenomenon may be received in multifarious ways by different species, we might begin to touch on the extension of this: the vast, intricate interconnectedness that is as much a fact of the world as any kind of separateness. The natural world is literally built by relationships. This is very difficult to grasp within a materialist philosophy, because relations between physical things can only be secondary to the things themselves. However, in a discussion of symbiotic relationships among different species, Hoffmeyer explains that "relationships and not individual species are carriers of causality".[4] At a completely different level, the development of different cell types in humans, which cell type any individual cell within an early embryo ultimately becomes is determined by its position within the whole. Thus, even though a cell is always a semi-autonomous system in itself, it is also shaped by relations. The cause of its "destiny" is positional, or its relationship to the whole.[5]

The concept of *umwelt* may be gaining traction. Damasio makes a similar observation when he explains that the special sense organs sample and describe aspects of the surrounding world, adding: "Fortunately, all of us are immersed in this same incompletely sampled "reality",[6] although for Damasio "in good part we share that level playing field with other species."[7] Many of Barrett's points about the construction of emotions resonate with it: "We do not passively detect physical changes in the world. We actively participate in constructing our experiences even though we are mostly unaware of the fact."[8] Barrett does make passing reference to "regularities" in the world a number of times, but without providing much explanation. Ultimately though she emphasises constructedness so much that actual engagement with the surrounding world is downplayed, to the point where the importance of relations seems to go missing. Thus:

> Your perceptions are so vivid and immediate that they compel you to believe that you experience the world *as it is*, when you actually experience a world *of your own construction.*[9]

Barrett partly gets around this by distinguishing between social reality (which is real but only for humans) and physical reality (which is real in a different way; it is *perceiver-independent*). As discussed in earlier chapters, it is very difficult to make sense of these points without examining underlying speculative assumptions. For now, it is worth noticing that biosemiotics moves beyond the distinction between physical and social reality. For biosemiotics, relationships permeate the natural world and are fundamentally causal. Moreover, biosemiotics is already based on a process metaphysics so it aligns with the speculative schema of this book. The purpose of aligning all of these concepts is that the theory as a whole will eventually help us to preserve and clarify some of Barrett's points while shifting the overall perspective from *constructedness* to *interconnectedness*. One of the most important aspects of this shift is that it will enable us to acknowledge the importance of the notion of attunements. We don't have magic brains that construct entire worlds for us. We have evolved into systems with a high degree of freedom and individuality because they are also deeply and subtly attuned to all kinds of regularities in the natural world, including other human beings. This is true for *all living organisms*, to greater and lesser degrees.

Barrett explains the generation of ordered perceptions in terms of the brain's ability to learn statistically; "a fundamental ability to learn from regularities and probabilities around you".[10] We should note that this learning is understood as overlaid on "the "blooming, buzzing confusion" that is really out there"[11] (here quoting William James' famous phrase). This misunderstands that fact that the natural world is highly ordered and learning is better expressed as an attunement to this order, rather than the creation of order out of complete disorder. Relations to the world need to become ordered through human development but many processes of the world itself are stable and repeating as are the evolutionary processes that give development its inner momentum, otherwise there would be no world and no human beings to inhabit it. Hoffmeyer makes this point in an interesting way in relation to Peirce's philosophy:

> In opposition to the natural science of his time,
> Peirce considered *indeterminacy* and *chance* as the
> primordial condition of the world. Given this
> starting point, the real "mystery to be unravelled"
> about our world is not so much that it contains an
> unbelievable mass of ungovernable activity, but
> that there is any stable order in it, at all.[12]

This is why understanding evolution is so important, to understand how the form of human selves, with its inner aspect of feeling and consciousness, came to be created and recreated through the long, slow process of evolution through many forms of selves. Here in turn is where the concept of final causation (the tendency toward end states) is crucial.

Final Causation

One way to approach the question of final causation is this: why did I as a fertilized egg and then an embryo become an adult human and not a sparrow or a frog? How can we describe this causally? These questions are conventionally answered in mainstream biology by positing that the fertilized egg that would eventually become me contained within it a set of instructions, the genetic material of my DNA, to make me as I am. But as discussed, instructions cannot exist separately from a system that interprets them. They only *become* instructions within a dynamic process of interpretation and are in no way an *agent* or *director*. In fact, Hoffmeyer remarks upon "the well-known chemical fact that DNA molecules are essentially passive under normal physiological conditions"[13] as well as the rather awkward finding, early in the twenty-first century, that the human genome contains very few uniquely human genes. Only a few hundred of its 30,000 genes are significantly different from those found in other mammals, such as mice. Genes simply do not *code for* particular traits. Cases in which a single gene relates directly to a particular condition (such as cystic fibrosis) are by far the exception, not the norm.[14] The idea of a gene as a *replicator*, popularised by the biologist Richard Dawkins, able to reproduce itself is highly misleading. A gene, by itself, does not *do* anything.

Instead, Hoffmeyer provides a description of the role of genes in developmental processes as much more dependent on and entwined with other processes, mostly inside but also beyond the cell, such that it is better to understand genes as *signposts* in an unfolding process rather than as causes or blueprints.[15] The whole process of development is directional but certainly not determined by genes alone. Embryonic cells diverge into different types of cells depending on their spatial position in the whole, and then cell lines respond differently to the genetic material they each contain, which is the same in different cells. The process of *transcription* during which the DNA is copied into the usable RNA that is then released from the nucleus into the cell's cytoplasm involves steps that are in themselves dynamic and interpretive, such as *editing* to recognise and remove so-called junk molecules. The *translation* processes that follow RNA copying before new proteins are formed and delivered wherever they are needed in the cell or excreted from the cell then involve many complicated steps through various structures within the cell. These processes are interactive and communicative. Thus, Hoffmeyer suggests the metaphor of genes as a computerised inventory control system comprised of menus for different applications. Which menus are available depends partly upon the cell type (its history) and so-called *decisions* as to which applications should be launched are a function of the cell as a whole system. In Hoffmeyer's words, these genetic pathways are a function of the "intricate semiotic *interplay of the total cellular system*".[16]

> ...it is precisely the subtle, never-ending interplay
> between the nucleus and these internal
> membranous structures that makes the cell a
> holistic organizational unit in itself. In the absence
> of these differentiated structures and their
> functions, the genomic specifications would not
> make any sense.[17]

Something very interesting arises here: the difference between the actual complexity of processes of development and the role of genes in them, and the more commonplace ideas about genes—which Hoffmeyer aptly summarises as "the fetishisation of the gene as a kind of self-replicating controller"—in many ways parallels debates about where agency exists in the whole human being. The ideas about genes that are currently more popular are based on the same metaphors as ideas about brains. They are master regulators acting out of blind self-interest. Not only that, the potential for changing difficult aspects of human life (for brains bad experiences, for genes physical diseases or perhaps, eventually, simply characteristics we do not like) lies in somehow replacing the wrong instruction. This fantasy does not even begin to grapple with the real nuances and interconnectedness of human beings with each other and with the natural world. Such a gap in our understanding should compel us to discover more about how life actually is *before* we make interventions, lest our interventions reveal the blunt tools of our materialist concepts in unforeseen, destructive ways.

Importantly, this does not mean that genes, as with brains, do not have any special function. Biosemiotics acknowledges their unique status. While genes do not *instruct* development they play a key role in the whole process. This overall process is well described as *self-calibration*. Recall that biosemiotics understands life as based on the capacity of a system to identify itself, or self-reference. Genes provide a very stable tool for self-reference in the process of development as well as through the life span as the system continually renews itself at the cellular level. Biosemiotics incorporates all the theories of self-organising systems explained in the previous chapter but also offers tools for understanding that a defining aspect of life is that it continues through generations. Thus, genes are stable descriptions that can be passed down a lineage. They act as a structure in relation to the dynamic process of cellular activity and replication. In keeping with the speculative schema, we can also say that the lineage is a process in itself. As such a dynamic process, the lineage is a process of separating and recombining that takes place over numerous generations, a much longer time frame than an individual life span.[18]

Analog and digital codes

Biosemiotics includes the concepts of change as either analog or digital, depending on perspective, which was introduced in the previous chapter.[19] These concepts are also used more specifically in relation to the conditions for life, which are also the conditions for self-reference. Thus, biosemiotics proposes that life depends upon the presence of *two codes*; one analog and one digital. In a living organism, the analog code is the dynamic process of the cell while the digital code is the genetic material. Hoffmeyer mentions that the use of the term *code* has caused some confusion. While the notion of genes as a digital code seems fairly straightforward, the idea of an analog code is less so. These problems are well resolved in relation to Peircean semiotics, but beyond the scope of the discussion here. However, we should note that the contemporary Western obsession with digital codes (genes, neurons, words, computer systems) often means that actual dynamic processes (cells, bodies, interactions, interfaces) are not seen as particularly relevant or even particularly causal. The term *analog code* simply makes clearer that dynamics have causal, or relational, effects. The cellular processes and the body as a whole are active interpreters that also influence gene expression or brain responses and the two, analog and digital, only really make sense in relation to each other, as a whole system.

The concepts of analog and digital codes might be easier to grasp if we use the term *description* instead of code. We have seen that the need for two descriptions of any phenomenon is a fundamental speculative assumption, because any phenomenon exists for itself as well as in relation to all else surrounding it. The creation of interiority, of life, which can also be described as containing change, begins with the double relation of an internal description. We can describe the developing cell or embryo as a dynamic process, as well as in two relations; to the genes and to the present environment. Final causes, the tendency towards end states that characterises development through the life span, require both of these relations. Life, as inward development and eventually consciousness, can be described as dynamic (driven by energy exchanges in the present moment, or efficient causes) and relational (also causally reliant on the initial structure of genes, or formal causes). The two of these together describe final causes; we change and develop over time, both as humans and as individuals. This contained change with its partially predictable momentum, which characterises life, can be described as a *special case of closure* that makes life different from other kinds of natural systems. Seen in terms of the scalar hierarchy that characterises dynamic systems in a present moment, life occurs when the long, slow process of genetic change through the lineage comes together with the much faster dynamic processes of the cell. Potentially, we can describe life as the coming together of *vastly different time scales in dynamic relation to one another*. The very different rates of change make opening inward possible, as new levels of complexity develop in between the level of the genes and the level of the cell or organism as a whole.

The idea of a special case of closure refers primarily to the fertilised egg as the beginning of life; conception is when the two time scales come together. But it is important to acknowledge that this situation is not the only form of replication through generations. At the other extreme end of the spectrum of life, bacteria (single-celled prokaryotic organisms) engage in a much more free form of DNA exchange than the sexual reproduction that characterises most animal and plant forms, at least at some point in their life cycles. Small fragments of DNA are easily exchanged among different species of bacteria, which then become active and take over the dynamic processes of the cell in certain environmental conditions, such as when growth is inhibited. In some few instances this will result in a helpful adjustment to an environmental stressor. This ability to exchange DNA combines with the sheer numbers of bacteria present on earth to make new, effective strains a likely outcome of chance mutations, explaining why bacteria are able to change and become resistant to antibiotics relatively quickly in evolutionary terms. Interestingly, the strategy for survival of bacteria that makes them so interwoven with each other genetically means that a single bacterium is a very different kind of individual than, say, a human being. The individual of a bacterial species might be better described at a different level, with a given species or even all bacteria more accurately understood as "short lived units in a huge global organism".[20]

Even within this example, the time scales of genetic change and dynamic cellular function do remain different enough to maintain the life of a single bacterium for a time; the lifespan of bacteria can range from twelve minutes to twenty-four hours.[21] However, the individual at this level is very generalised, which supports the idea that the slower the process of genetic change, the more potential exists for opening inward once the genes become involved in the dynamics of a cell. In multicellular organisms this increases again. The stable, repeating processes of development within a species means that individual cells differentiate into different cell lines very early in the process, but the loss of freedom (or constraint) at this level supports much more freedom and individuation at the level of the whole organism. Even though genes are just one tool in the larger process of multicellular life, it is important to reiterate their unique status. The transition to life is not a gradual one; life requires a minimal level of complexity. The smallest number of genes necessary for life, currently identified in a species of bacteria *Mycoplasma genitalium*, is around five hundred.[22]

Genes and language

Biosemiotics considers genes and language as two examples of digital codes. One important feature they have in common is that they both introduce new possibilities for novelty, because within their own reshuffling they are unconstrained by the demands of the natural world. They do not need to fit with reality, to immediately find their place in the dynamic interconnectedness, in the same way that organisms as a whole need to. Thus, both genetic recombining and language are free to produce impossible combinations. For genes this simply means new combinations that will *not* work. But the possibility for unworkable rearrangements is the very condition for creativity, for the generation of new forms that *will* work especially in new contexts in an ever-changing environment.

Language is similar. It allows for conjecture, for what *might* be as well as for describing what is *not* present or does *not* exist, thus opening up new creative paths. In this light, metaphor is a fascinating phenomenon. By structuring our understanding of one experience in terms of another, metaphor occupies a position in between the notion of what *is* and what *is not*; but where there is a connecting factor that allows the metaphor to make sense, such as the characteristic unfolding over time of *journeys* and *relationships*, or that *more* of something often coincides with its level going *up* in space. Of course, people may try out new metaphors but for them to be meaningful to others and to persist over time requires that they interact creatively with our potential experience in some way. In this way, metaphors resemble *umwelt*. They produce a stable relationship to something, although that *something* might be our own experience rather than some phenomenon outside of ourselves, which is the way we would usually consider a creature's *umwelt*. The important point here is that metaphor creatively elaborates our experience. It is the basis of genuinely emergent novelty but not unrelated to phenomena of the world, other people or ourselves. And now we can see, hopefully, that genetic change functions in a similar way. Whether it becomes information in a dynamic, interpretive process or not relates as much to the surrounding cellular, multicellular and broader dynamic processes as to the molecular recombination in itself.

> Chance mutations are not selected because they are
> beneficial; they are beneficial because they happen
> to appear in a relational system which was already
> well prepared for them. That blind selection should
> be the sole cause of evolution is one of the
> mightiest fictions of our time. Selection is never
> blind; it is always guided by the prior formation of
> developmental and semiotic integration.[23]

Thus, Hoffmeyer quotes the biologist François Jacob, who proclaimed that "Evolution is a process of tinkering rather than of engineering."[24] This statement echoes, once again, an important aspect of processes of cognition. *Tinkering* is the same term Barrett uses to describe the process by which the brain weighs the importance of different types of information before producing a stable perception or action. Tinkering, in both evolution and cognition, seems to be all about exploring within ranges of possibility, to *find the best fit* through *subtle processes of attunement*. It has so far been a rather long road from the introductory discussion of Barrett's theory of emotion simply to explain that tinkering, or attunement, in both unconscious and conscious cognitive processes deserves much more exploration. But the purpose has been to offer a context for this claim; a full and consistent speculative theory of nature. Of course, my intention has also been to debunk the notion of the brain as a controller, at the same time as demonstrating the strength of this metaphor in contemporary culture. We do tend to think of causal processes as involving a controller that directly causes an effect. All of the theory provided so far—from the speculative categories through the complexity theories to the biosemiotic view of genetics and evolution—also leads to a key insight to keep in mind from here on: the causal processes by which metaphor shapes our experience and understanding are not unique to language or to humans. They take the same form as all kinds of change in nature and we can identify and observe them at many different biological levels, albeit only from the outside. As Hoffmeyer states "We are, so to speak, historically formed by the world—and this is basically why we can learn to know it."[25]

PART 3

BEHAVIOUR, EMOTION, AND FEELING

8

Behaviour as best fit

UNDERSTANDING THE FUNCTIONING of hierarchical systems, particularly living, semi-autonomous systems, should provide us with some important background insights for understanding the emergence of consciousness in nature, and eventually feeling as humans experience it. One such insight is that processes of attunement, which are said to occur in the brain as competing interpretations of situations, occur all the way down the scalar hierarchy. Levels are dynamically separate but in causal relation to one another and that relation must remain within a range that ensures enough stability for the system to survive over time. Ranges of adjustment and response can occur in relation to lower level, environmental or developmental changes and, as biosemiotics explains so clearly, these processes almost always involve the interpretation of signs. Thus, what can look like decision-making or agency should be understood in a different way; as emergent interpretations that demonstrate the complex intricacy of evolution and the vast timescale that it is has required. It is tempting to name this intricacy *intelligence,* but this is too easily misread as anthropomorphic or idealist. Perhaps we could describe the world as it has emerged through evolution as an exquisitely detailed web of interwoven change. However we see it, attunement and interpretation are basic to nature and this helps us to begin to imagine how complex processes emerge in relation to other complex processes but do not require anything like our human consciousness. Genes are an excellent example. Seeing them as controllers or instructors seems inadequate in the context of more dynamic explanations that account for their participation in active cellular processes, along with their considerable stability in relation to these.

Seeing nature as permeated by causal relationships and communicative processes has a paradoxical effect. By acknowledging the complexity of all processes, and especially processes that we characterise as living, the complexity of human life remains remarkable but no longer unique. We are more obviously embedded in the world, as the enactivist approach to embodied cognition claims. Here it is worth briefly recalling the points made earlier about the notion of representation in the brain. Focusing on processes of attunement, whether inside or outside a body or a brain, could very well mean that we eventually no longer need the concept of representation at all. This might even be a fairly simple follow-on from no longer seeing the brain as an agent or decision maker. However, the effects of this on ideas about consciousness and choice are also paradoxical; attunement is more immediate but also seems less free. But attunement also ascribes much less agency to unconscious processes and, as we will eventually see, gives us more tools to expand and work with that which is conscious.

At the same time we need to keep in mind one of the problematic tendencies of enactivism, that focusing on present-time attunements to an environment or how processes cross borders of body, brain and world de-emphasises the highly internalised nature of any semi-autonomous system. Thus, we need to see unconscious processes as formed over time (both evolutionarily and in the formation of a self in an individual life) and productive of adjustments in relation to an environment, but without placing ultimate agency in these processes. A discussion of behaviour will build on this point.

Behaviour

The fact that processes at much lower levels, indeed most natural processes, are complex gives us good reason to observe behaviour *before* we make inferences about possible inner experiences. The inner aspect/outer aspect schema is relevant here. While all observation is a choice and thereby involves the paradox of differentiation, we nonetheless find that our relations to many aspects of the natural, physical world are very stable. We can be systematic in our observations and gather reliable results from this. Thus, observing the behaviour of any living whole, such as plants and animals and even people, is not in principle different from observing lower level physiology or even biochemical reactions, even though living wholes may be considered more complex processes because more internal levels of change are present.

Granted, if we create entire theories about consciousness or experience by observing behaviour alone we tend towards something like behaviourism. Depending on which version, behaviourism may be based on a *method* of observing behaviour alone to understand psychology or on the *idea* that we can and/or should explain all mental concepts with reference to behaviour.[1] Gallagher mentions that enactivist approaches to cognition have been criticised as a version of behaviourism but answers this criticism with a distinction between mere behaviour and intentional action; complex behaviour has a purposive structure that includes intention and makes it action. Interestingly, Barrett also mentions behaviourism—now seen by some as a "notorious" epoch within the field of psychology[2]—in her critique of the essentialist view of emotion. But her criticism of behaviourism's lack of concern for actual experience seems very similar to the problems I have with her constructionist account of emotion, because experience becomes somehow erroneous, unimportant or too disconnected from the world.

The speculative schema can explain something important here, although it may seem obvious in hindsight. Any neuroscientific description is of a lower level than the whole body, therefore one of many lower level processes constitutive of the whole process of the self. We are not in it and we can therefore only observe it from the outside. So if particular, repeatable processes can be observed in a time scale that precedes but is close to consciousness, they may be so-called unconscious processes but we only infer this because we can only observe them in relation and from the outside.

There is simply no such phenomenon as unconscious experience. Unconscious *processes* might be physically within us (as lower level constitutive processes) but they are also in important respects outside us. Even observing our own behaviour is a perspective from the outside when we differentiate it from our experience. There are, however, ways in which we can notice experience arising and dissipating, and different ways we can interact with our own experience. Some of these seem to bring us very close to the border of consciousness, or even different kinds of consciousness, and perhaps therefore the processes that constitute consciousness, albeit always in relation to what is happening around us and to our particular histories. But before we attempt to directly observe experience, *and we can each only observe our own*, it is worth being as systematic as possible in observing from the outside; in other words, developing concepts for understanding behaviour. Hoffmeyer recognises this inside/outside relationship when he remarks:

> The error of confusing first-person experience and
> third-person experience is widespread in much
> 'scientific' thinking.[3]

Indeed, this might be nowhere as pronounced as in the interpretation of fMRI results. Hoffmeyer cites a newspaper headline that reads: "SCIENTISTS WILL SOON BE ABLE TO SEE CONSCIOUSNESS".[4]

Neuroscientific explanations, if taken alone and assumed to offer complete explanations of experience, look like behaviourism, albeit translated into physiology.

Hoffmeyer says this, which we can relate to behaviour:

> But even though science might not need to concern itself with examining the inner side of subjectivity, it may and should be concerned with examining the external side of subjectivity, such as the question of how the possession of subjectivity affects the living systems under study. It is not the task of biology to say what animal experiences are like (considered *as experiences*), but it is the task of biology to deal with the fact that at least some animals *have* experiences, and to study how this affects their livelihood.[5]

In the terms already being used here, Hoffmeyer is referring to the importance of observing how animals attune to their surroundings in ways that help them to survive and flourish. Starting here with behaviour before turning to experience, including feeling, also preserves the important orientation of speculative naturalism—namely to begin with theories of nature and to thoroughly accommodate the natural sciences. This is also the justification for the explanations of natural systems in earlier chapters.

We might consider that inner experience like our human consciousness has occurred relatively recently in evolutionary terms without necessarily giving up the possibility that earlier or apparently simpler evolutionary forms have an inner development that is *something*, albeit unknowable to us. This something may or may not require a nervous system; we do not know. What we can see, from the outside, is that living systems engage with their environments in all sorts of complex ways to maintain and develop themselves. In animals the most obvious of these is movement, or motility. One of the simplest forms of motility is moving the whole organism towards what is beneficial and away from what is harmful. Even a single celled organism will move towards food sources and away from environmental toxins. Importantly, a single-celled organism can also demonstrate learning, such as a slime mould that will learn to recognize a previously unknown chemical as harmless once it has encountered it without ill effect just a few times.[6] This fulfills the criteria that living systems collect historical information through their life span and that this may take the form of shifts in functioning, for instance the speed with which the slime mould crosses the chemical to reach a food source. Even though this type of learning (termed habituation) might also be undone relatively quickly, such shifts are memory and physiology at the same time; an identifiable process occurs in double relation, to present and past. The creation of such interiority, with or without an inner aspect or consciousness like ours, is the definition of a living system.

Plants also exhibit movements that could easily be described as behaviour, such as the rotation of leaves towards or away from the sun. The phenomenologist Stephen Strasser notes that some human behaviours are similar to this. We also act to maximise or diminish surface area. We wrap our arms in when we are cold and stretch out in warmth. Strasser considers that behaviours such as "the self-extension and stretching of a man comfortably sunning himself"[7] should be considered plant-like rather than animalistic, expanding our sense of evolutionary connectedness and of what counts as behaviour. Even the growth patterns of plants can be seen to constitute a kind of behaviour. Recent treatises on the interconnectedness of trees[8] have been hugely popular, prompting us to imagine intentionalities such as care and attention in the behaviours of trees. Unsurprisingly, some scientists have lamented this anthropomorphising.[9] But we have already seen how biosemiotics, with its focus on communication via signs at all levels, provides a path between the two extremes of intention and mechanistic reacting. So much happens in the natural world before we need assume an intentionality *like ours*, but at the same time the natural world is replete with purpose. In fact, purpose is intimately tied with final causation.

The concept of the act

If we want to emphasise the commonalities of behaviour and physiology, and perhaps even less complex or non-organic reactions in nature, we need to find concepts that provide common ground for such apparently different activities. In other words, we need a way to demarcate specific processes that holds across many levels. The philosopher Suzanne Langer's concept of the *act* accomplishes this; acts are recognizable elements in the dynamism of life. The concept of the act is in important respects amenable to the speculative schema, in particular the dialectic of differentiation. It is a perspective on "the continuum of a life" yet demarcates acts as "peaks of activity which are centres of recognizable phases".[10] Langer elaborates, acts:

> normally show a phase of acceleration, or
> intensification of a distinguishable dynamic
> pattern, then reach a point at which the pattern
> changes, whereupon the movement subsides.[11]

One of the most important aspects of Langer's characterization of acts is their reliance on phases of tension and release:

> What gives every act its indivisible wholeness is that
> its initial phase is the building up of tension, a store of
> energy which has to be spent; all subsequent phases
> are modes of meting out that charge, and the end of
> the act is the complete resolution of the tension.[12]

According to Langer, this form of the act applies to all human and animal movements, as well as to lower level processes:

> In plants as in animals, the vital activities subsume
> smaller and smaller events, yet biologists still
> recognize the basic indivisible act form, even when
> they are delving down to the biochemical factors
> involved in those complex processes.[13]

Of course this is a rather neat definition; the act has a definable initial phase, some period of activity and a resolution. But even if acts are built up and set off in more complex ways, interrupted in their duration or reinforced so that they continue on to new acts, such situations should be seen as variations of this more simple form. Any given act that we observe is also completely relational; Langer accounts for the fullness of change with the idea that every act arises from a situation. This fits very well with the way that levels and hierarchies were explained. Any discernible process that arises occurs in relation to constituents and constraints as well as, in principle, the wholeness of change. As change occurs, say, in an environment, some recognition of this change occurs across borders between levels, sometimes via material or energetic exchange but most often via semiosis. Disturbance occurs, which we can also name as lack of attunement. The build up of energy within a given level simply *is* this lack of attunement, which increases until the process changes to release the energetic charge in a way that reattunes the organism, or restores harmony amongst levels.

Sometimes the build up is more obviously in lower levels (such as physiological energy requirements) that may require behaviour to resolve it (such as seeking food and eating). Here the behaviour of the whole body is the emergent level that resolves lower level disturbance. This behaviour occurs in relation to all kinds of rhythms already evolutionarily set to a range in animals, as well as elaborated in an individual life. At other times, emergent behaviour occurs in relation to impingements that are more obviously environmental, say the appearance of a predator. The build up in this case is very quick; emergent action can be almost immediate. The concept of the act as holistic helps us to understand whole situations. We do not necessarily need to distinguish between the perception of the predator and the following response. The build up *is* the perception and not separable from the whole act of fleeing or fighting; the build up is a phase of the whole act and it must be released somehow. Langer's relational view of perception is relevant here: for animals, objects and their qualities "enter into their perceptual acts only as they enter into their overt behaviour as values for action".[14] Here, values for action refers clearly to interpretation, just as biosemiotics describes.

Concepts such as motivation also become more relational in this view; motivation is a phase of build up within a whole act. Of course sometimes an internal pressure builds at a lower level that does not result in action. Langer names this early phase, one that has the potential to set off a complete act, an *impulse.* There may be numerous competing impulses at lower levels. The impulse is described as "a homogenous discharge of energy, the equivalent in animate nature of a force".[15] It provides an internal pressure towards the completion of an act. That a given impulse may or may not lead to a complete behavioural act preserves the sense of the whole body behavioural level as emergent, and thereby interpretive and always potentially creative. Animal behaviour is better seen as deeply relational than mechanistically triggered.

Of course, much animal behaviour is evolutionarily prepared, as instinctual acts. Langer outlines a number of species-specific acts of varying complexity, from the simplest "pure reflexes" through to "apparently purposeful, elaborate acts".[16] But, here again, instinct does not mean mechanistically triggered. Instinctual acts may be intelligently performed or felt: "Animal intelligence is the perception of opportunities to perform instinctive acts without suffering any harm."[17] Obviously simpler behaviours, such as reflexes, seem more automatic than more complex forms of engagement, but it is difficult to see why we should ever view them as completely mechanistic, given that even the simplest relations to an environment can be modified through the life span, as early forms of learning and memory. However, it may be true that the possibility for organisms to evolve the capacity for more complex forms of behaviour rests on less complex forms of response becoming more habitual, repetitive or set in that particular species. New forms of engagement do not emerge preformed from nowhere, but rely on what the species, or for that matter the individual animal, has already been able to do. This point also highlights that the corporeal form of any animal *simply is* its various forms of physiology and *whole body behaviours* as seen from the outside. The body is a form of activity seen at a particular level. This is why we should resist the idea of some system or organ of the body *instructing* other systems or organs of the body to action. An instruction is really an initial phase of a whole act and arises in relation to a whole situation, inside and outside the body. And even though in humans perceived opportunities for various kinds of engagement with other people and an environment are heavily influenced by learning and memory, and thereby seem to originate within an individual, there are a multitude of possibilities for their emergence at various levels of functioning. Such possibilities may be ascribable to memory but they also cut across divisions of brain and body.

Best fit and harmony

The point of this description of behaviour is to emphasise that sustaining life in semi-autonomous systems relies on the maintenance of harmony amongst levels internal to the organism and of the whole organism in its environment. As with the play of order and disorder, disharmony is as necessary as harmony for creative elaboration, in evolution and in an individual life. Life depends on a fine balance of the two and on the possibility of each remaining within an appropriate range. If an opportunity to engage in behaviour to reharmonise is not available it is more likely that disharmony be accommodated at lower levels than that it explode into greater misattunement with an environment. An extreme example of this in the world of vertebrates is the freeze response. When survival is threatened and opportunities are not available for fighting or fleeing, the whole body enters into a state of paralysis. An enormous build up of tension is contained until such opportunity arises or the animal is killed. Again, there does not need to be any consciousness of these choices, but still the response itself can be quite realistically considered an attunement to a whole situation. Moreover, this attunement can be seen as a genuine understanding, even without anything like our human consciousness. Thus, even in the most extreme circumstances, an organism seeks the best fit between internal impulses, tensions and compulsions, whether or not there is any conscious awareness of these impulses, tensions and compulsions as such. But if behaviour is the highest emergent level, or the whole body, from the outside, then we can surmise that this whole from the inside is *some kind of phenomenon* that is different from lower level processes.

This reiterates once again the point made so well in biosemiotics; a species' *umwelt* depends on a real relation to the world outside, often including other organisms of the same species. The metaphor of the hallucinating brain simply doesn't make sense. In fact, evolutionarily speaking the situation may be the opposite of hallucination. Hoffmeyer discusses an important point about morphological complexity that is easily overlooked if we exclude semiosis, or communication and interpretation, from nature. After a certain point in evolution (possibly the Devonian period, three to four hundred million years ago) morphological complexity in animals doesn't increase. In other words, the bodies of animals after a certain level are not more complex, just different. That the number of genes also doesn't appreciably increase is further evidence of this. What does change, however, is the complexity of semiotic engagement. Evolution is as much the elaboration of forms of relationship and communication as of the living forms in themselves. In this context brains, and particularly human brains with their capacity for language, support an obvious increase in complexity. But the semiosis that brains help humans to accomplish—essentially finer and finer forms of discrimination and awareness of relations to the world and to other people—is a *decrease* in distance, not the increase that hallucination suggests. We are closer to each other and the world, not further away; this is in some ways the paradox of our individuation. A high degree of individuation is only possible with the *counterbalance* of ways to understand and engage.

Even without consciousness as we know it, all behaviour demonstrates a best fit for the organism at that time and incorporates its history of interactions; the double relation. This view of behaviour is quite similar to Barrett's in many respects, although the underlying theory and therefore the language by which we express it is very different. According to Barrett, the brain generates many hypotheses about situations and how we should deal with them and then selects a winning instance based on calculations involving similar instances in the past. However an *idea* of *what happened last time* is a projection back from what is more conscious. We can relate to this because we often problem solve by explicitly thinking through scenarios and remembering what happened in other similar scenarios. But the emergence of this conscious ability in humans is a follow on from the ability to attune generally, which requires the whole of evolution. Processes within hierarchical semi-autonomous systems express what has worked before by virtue of their very existence. We do not need to posit a special *interest* in the maintenance of the system or homeostasis (or preferably homeorhesis, to include the system's trajectory) by one feature of the system. The so-called interest is deeply built into the possibility of its being there and being able to identify itself at many levels. Survival and flourishing are always paramount, which follows naturally from self-identification. Langer also recognises this when she says that "An organism always does everything it can."[18] This makes much more sense in relation to a view of nature as fundamentally creative at the deepest level; it is difficult to understand without it. But if we do assume this—and we must always assume at least one basic fact about the world—we can see that living systems are always opening within limits, finding the edges of what is possible, sometimes succeeding and sometimes failing. Of course, our humans brains *do* appear to be intricately involved in our possibilities for finer discriminations in the world, and indeed in ourselves, but we do not need to see the physical brain as somehow calculating or selecting. Each new level of order is the harmonising within limits, just as all levels of order before and below any given level have done and continue to do.

Even so, harmonising levels within a self is useless without harmonising levels outside of a self through real relations; that is what harmonising means. So interest in others and a surrounding world is as much a requirement for survival and flourishing as self-interest. If the world, most basically defined as change, is indeed fundamentally creative, then the level of separateness of a living system such as a human being (generated through long processes of evolution and detailed processes of individuation within a life) exists reciprocally with all the ways we can meet the world, the fineness of our potential for experiences of beauty, love, desire, connection, openness. These depend on relations that are at once real and creative and do not at all mean that we should disregard the survival imperatives of homeostasis and interoception, in which there is currently great scientific interest. But we should see that these processes support, constitute and buffer many other processes that emerge at the level of the whole self that we *do* experience, notably always within the basic fact that we want to stay alive but that we only will, as individuals, for a limited amount of time.

9

Nonconscious behaviour and implicit memory

OUR CONSIDERATION OF complex behaviours and interactions that permeate the natural world *before* assuming anything about consciousness or inner awareness should simply highlight that behaviour is a form of understanding that we can observe from the outside. Actions, as attunements to situations, express forms of understanding, developed through evolution or an individual life, or usually to some extent both. Any kind of elaboration of behaviour involves memory, even if it results from simpler forms of learning such as habituation or conditioning. Thus, we can even suggest that when we observe organisms, particularly animals, doing almost anything we are observing their memories as well as their present-time behaviours, which are at once individual and species-specific. Many levels of functioning occur before these processes are separated, especially into the explicitly conscious forms of learning and memory that humans engage in and can talk about. The background of biosemiotics clarifies that these explicit human forms are continuous with the communication and interpretation that occurs throughout nature. But, importantly, biosemiotics also allows that language is a highly and perhaps uniquely successful form of semiosis.

The concept of the act offers a way of grasping that behaviour, a process viewed from the outside, is in important respects like any other natural process. This helps us to identify that the whole body acting is a different level than any other within an organism, which is crucial for reflecting on neuroscience and its extrapolations. The act helps us to keep wholeness in mind. Even so, the act, as it was presented in the previous chapter, is a somewhat simplified concept. It may not be straightforward to identify boundaries of particular acts. For example, web building is a characteristic behaviour of many species of spider. From one perspective we can view this behaviour (say, an individual spider spinning a single web) as a whole form. It involves a sequence of steps towards a completed whole, and does not require that the spider is conscious of or reflects on the structure emerging from its behaviour. The fact that sometimes when a spider is moved part-way through the building process, it will resume where it left off and generate a partial structure seems to support metaphors such as a genetic code or behavioural program in the DNA or neurons of the spider. However, spiders will adjust to changing conditions in a multitude of situations; they are able to finish webs already partially built by another spider, to detect and replace missing rays in a web and to build differently sized webs adapted to local conditions.[1] Very fine adjustments in relation to situations are within the possibility of web building. This raises the point that the whole act may be formed of smaller subunits which may also be seen as whole acts, when we choose to focus on them this way. But even more importantly, the degree of adjustment to conditions possible in even this paradigmatic, species-specific behaviour suggests an ongoing attunement of different levels of change, in this case inside and outside the spider as a whole organism. This fitting or harmonising does not require a consciousness that resembles our human perceptions or understanding of the whole situation, but at the same time it is highly responsive such that we might consider it a form of understanding.

The point of being careful to think about animal behaviour in this way is to be able to think differently about conscious and unconscious behaviour in human beings, and the groundwork for this is a more accurate distinction between emotion and feeling. The purpose is not ultimately to deny consciousness and feeling in animals but to open up the possibilities for imagining it, without assuming that we can ever directly know how it is. At the same time, such possibilities should in turn, in later chapters, enable us to reflect differently on our own conscious experiences.

To restate an important point about the individuation of organisms as living systems: the balance and interplay of separating from while also coming into contact with the surrounding world needs to generate a best fit for the continuity of the system, for survival. The seeking of best fit must be a creative process in itself. To follow through our example: web building behaviour is both a dynamic contact (because it allows the spider to access the world, including sources of food, in a particular way) and a separation (because the spider creates a new structure while adding to its behavioural repertoire, even if only in small ways). All sorts of communication with the world are made possible through the web; for example webs support vibratory communication at a distance between males and females, thereby facilitating approach behaviours for sexual reproduction.[2] As we have already seen, this dynamic creation of new relations is well handled by biosemiotics and, at a fundamental level, by the speculative schema.

Wakefulness and effort

Hans Jonas, whose analysis of the development of materialism and idealism was discussed earlier, sees something similar to a fundamental creativity when he refers to the "primeval restlessless of metabolising substance". He also acknowledges that separation or individuation involves the creation of distance and that bridging this distance is central to animal life. "The great secret of animal life lies precisely in the gap which it is able to maintain between immediate concern and mediate satisfaction".[3] Movement, also fundamental to animal life, is key to bridging distance in space; moving towards or away from what is beneficial or harmful. However, more relevant to the present discussion is the idea of emotion as spanning distance in time. Referring to animal life, Jonas says:

> This precarious and exposed mode of living commits to wakefulness and effort, whereas plant life can be dormant. Responding to the lure of the prey, of which perception has given notice, alertness turns into the strain of pursuit and into the gratification of fulfilment, but it also knows the pang of hunger, the agony of fear, the anguished strain of flight. Pursuit itself may end in the disappointment of failure. In short, the indirectness of animal existence holds in its wakefulness the twin possibilities of enjoyment and suffering.[4]

This passage does something we have carefully avoided up until this point. It sees emotional experiences like our own in the experience of animals, when we cannot really know what it is like for the animal. At the same time, we can identify the arc of activity that is the act form—for instance from alertness through strain to gratification—at least somewhat in the behaviour itself. Even if we decide not to assume anything about the inner experience of the animal, the emotive language does convey something important about certain kinds of animal behaviour, namely its *strongly purposive* nature. This reminds again of Langer's statement that "An organism always does everything it can". It bridges the distance in the best way available at the time. This deeply purposive investment in its own life, where it will find and make use of opportunities to continue and to flourish, is something we *can* observe. We cannot see from the outside what it feels like to be a mouse or a hawk but we can observe this stretching towards limits within the precariousness of its very existence in behaviour. *Effort* is the basis for coming to understand emotion as a class of behaviour rather than a kind of inner experience.

Implicit and explicit appraisal

One distinction that enables reflection on emotion and its connection with behaviour is between implicit and explicit appraisal. Decision making, and by extension brain functioning, is often divided into two systems or realms: the implicit that is fast, automatic and unconscious (or nonconscious) and the explicit that is slow, deliberate and conscious. This distinction has been researched and applied particularly in relation to responses and experiences associated with fear. We can observe it in our own behaviour. The classic example is that of being startled by something dangerous (say, a snake) only to then realise that we were not actually in danger (say, because we mistook a bent stick in the grass for a snake). In this instance, we react before we consciously understand the situation, and for good reason; the ability to respond quickly and without awareness to certain kinds of situations has developed for survival and is evolutionarily built in. We can think of it as one of the earliest kinds of behaviour, retracting in the face of danger.

Unfortunately, this division appears to have become somewhat overused, simplifying the distinction between conscious and unconscious appraisal and at times seeing it as more strong or definite than it likely is. In his book *Anxious: Understanding the Brain to Treat Fear and Anxiety*, Joseph LeDoux, a leading neuroscientist in the study of emotion, discusses this problem. LeDoux began research into what he has previously termed the fear system of the brain in the mid-1980s. His earlier research into the involvement of particular brain areas (the amygdala and the thalamus) in various kinds of fear responses became well known for its distinction between two neural pathways, which he named the low road and the high road. In simple terms, certain neural connections between the thalamus and the amygdala are more direct than others and enable faster responses, such as jumping away from a snake; they prioritise speed over accuracy. The longer, slower pathway goes by way of the visual cortex, which means that it enables more fine-grained visual perceptions of objects and situations, and thereby supports more accurate appraisals of danger. While the low road/high road model applies to a genuine distinction in neural pathways and is supported by research with humans, the term low road came to be equated with nonconscious processing and the high road with conscious processing. In his more recent book, LeDoux is clear that both pathways are nonconscious: "the amygdala is a nonconscious processor of information from both roads".[5]

We should note that the concept of nonconscious processing can be confusing, because it is difficult to say if we are ever really *conscious* of any *processing* in the same way that we can be conscious of say, movement or feeling. LeDoux does recognise this, and gets around it by distinguishing processing and content, leaving an underlying dualism. Yet LeDoux also uses terms such as conscious and nonconscious processing because as a materialist (he uses the term *physicalist perspective*)[6] he understands consciousness as a phenomenon of the brain that will eventually be *fully* explained by physical, neural processes. Consciousness is "an intrinsic feature of a neural network with unique information representation capacities and made possible by unique patterns of connectivity".[7] In some respects it does seem that when we engage in conversation or deliberately think something through we are *conscious of* the process and thereby engaged in explicit processing, but this very direct, active kind of consciousness doesn't seem to be the usual way we are conscious in daily life. Indeed, LeDoux points out that even though we can separate implicit and explicit processes or systems in the brain— in principle and in experimental situations—in real life the two function at the same time, influence each other and may use the same resources. His emphasis is then much more on the implicit and nonconscious:

> In daily life naturally occurring cues that are fully
> visible or audible can bias our behaviour in
> complex ways that we have no knowledge of or
> conscious control over.[8]

Furthermore, as LeDoux also points out, neuroscientific studies have demonstrated that people will provide an explicit explanation for their behaviour in a situation even when they don't know what elicited it.[9] Of course, the notion that behaviour can be caused by processes that are not conscious (and be therefore in an important sense unconscious) is not particularly radical or new; Freudian psychoanalysis is a case in point. But they do appear to be supported by findings about different circuits or levels of processing in the brain. More importantly, though, LeDoux's increasing emphasis on implicit or nonconscious appraisal has meant that he has developed a strong position on animal consciousness. A major theme of *Anxious* is that a pervasive problem exists in the study of brain processes and behaviour, one that appears to result in part from the fact that much of the direct evidence of different neural pathways for different responses comes from experiments with animals, usually rats. This problem is that scientists will often refer to behaviours in animals (which can be observed) using the terms for emotions, such as fear (which are subjective states and cannot be observed). LeDoux argues that we should always attempt to explain behaviours without reference to conscious states and not assume conscious emotional experiences like ours, especially when we can explain them with reference to nonconscious processes alone. This is a similar point to that made in the previous chapter, and builds from the observation that terms for emotions are often used in ways that do not discriminate between behaviour and feeling states.

For LeDoux, developing a stronger position on animal consciousness has meant that he now uses the term *threat detection* rather than fear when referring to brain processes,[10] and he even states that threat detection is fundamentally nonconscious and implicit. Threat detection turns out not to be related to the functioning of one particular, identifiable system in the brain, but makes use of different circuits that relate to the kinds of behaviours they evoke. In a recent review paper LeDoux and Nathaniel Daw refer to a "new taxonomy of defensive behaviour",[11] which includes innate responses, such as reflexes and fixed reactions through to habits, goal directed actions and eventually deliberative actions. These different forms can be partly distinguished on the basis of how flexible responses are in relation to past experience. Most interesting is that LeDoux and Daw "consider that both human and nonhuman animals undertake elaborate, nonconscious forms of cognitive deliberation".[12] This means that complex actions can be planned and carried out without the human or animal being explicitly aware of the planning or the reason for the subsequent action. A subjective experience of fear is not necessary for this level of engagement. For these authors, when such an experience does occur, it *explicitly* motivates planned action; in this case, we are aware of fear and that we need to act to avoid or mitigate harm.

Implicit memory

LeDoux and Daw's taxonomy of behaviour makes very clear that complex behaviour can occur without explicit, conscious enagement—even *deliberation* can be implicit—which clearly supports the idea that what can look like decision-making or agency very often might be better described as an attunement to a situation. Moreover, that attunement expresses a double relation, to present circumstances and to individual history; it relies on learning and memory.

Once again, many of these processes are implicit or, as LeDoux says, "nonconscious all the way".[13]

> Many of the things we learn in life and use as we
> interact with our physical and social environment
> (such as syntactic parsing of sentences, depth
> perception, instrumentally reinforced actions, and
> habits) involve implicit, nonconscious processes and
> content to which we have no direct conscious access.[14]

Indeed, that many implicitly formed memories are expressed in the modality in which they were learnt (such as the memory of learning to ride a bike expressed in the activity of subsequently doing it) starts to break down the distinction between memory and physiology, particularly if we include the whole body in the process of learning and remembering.

Learning can be more or less automatic and elaborate. The more automatic forms usually come under umbrella terms for various kinds of conditioning, such as cued conditioning when a rat forms an association between a novel stimulus (such as a tone) and a stimulus that automatically elicits a response (such as freezing when a shock is administered). However, even at this relatively simple level of learning, context can be the basis for a learned association. A rat that freezes in response to being shocked in a particular chamber will freeze without the shock when placed in the same chamber but not when placed in a different chamber.[15] This is termed contextual conditioning. Without going into the many types of conditioning (which are very well explained in *Anxious,* as well as by LeDoux and Daw) it is worth noticing the underlying principle that a great deal of memory relies on *forming associations*. Even explicit memories that we can describe, in which a particular brain area (the hippocampus) is involved, can be understood as more elaborate associations. The hippocampus is said to store "relational memories",[16] which are involved in deliberation that may or may not be conscious. Even though the hippocampus is classically associated with explicit memory, LeDoux and Daw suggest that it may also be involved at a nonconscious level in flexible decision behaviours. Memory might be much less about specific objects or events but instead based on *the relations between them* or, as has already been suggested many times, whole situations. This fits entirely with the view in some fields of embodied cognition that perception itself is inherently relational. We learn to make finer discriminations from gestalt impressions rather than adding up separate details to form perceptions.

Global states

LeDoux is a neuroscientist who views consciousness as a neurally based phenomenon and the brain as a regulator or controller. In this respect his work is not aligned with the main arguments being made throughout this book. However, to reiterate one of this book's central goals, we can shift underlying theory and thereby some of the extrapolations from empirical research, without disagreeing with the empirical research itself or with definitions that are useful in some contexts, such as implicit and explicit. That certain, observable neural events correspond with types of behaviour, or even precede some behaviours, does not mean that we need to view the brain in this way. For example, LeDoux describes the systems for threat detection as defensive survival circuits, and says that they are present in most animals. The activation of these circuits results in a defensive motivational state, which LeDoux also terms a *global organismic state*. This is *an overall response of the body and brain*, which then guides further defensive responses. The brain and body become primed for additional defensive behaviours. LeDoux is careful to say that the defensive responses are not *caused by* motivational states, but rather that they *contribute to* them. This is compatible with the idea of perception itself as a response, the beginning of a whole act; the whole system shifts a certain way. If we see it this way it becomes more difficult to delineate where the response begins, and certainly once an act has begun it clearly emerges from the whole body, even if the brain continues to play a distinct role in the whole act. Furthermore, LeDoux's work is permeated with references to hierarchical organisation, yet the notion of circuits essentially engaging in complex computation does not leave much room for genuine creative elaboration and therefore misses something that, while mysterious, must be fundamental to hierarchical organisation: the emergence of new levels is creative. Thus, LeDoux and Daw consider:

> the notion that the brain has many routes for responding to threat raises a higher-level problem, which has also arisen repeatedly in our review: how do responses compete, and, more generally, how is the appropriate response for a given situation selected and adaptively deployed?[17]

The life cycle of a system and particularly the collection of historical information makes some sense of adaptive responses through an individual life. Attunements to situations become more refined until the system reaches a tipping point and responses become less flexible. But the refinements in themselves, which are also always relational, are only possible because the highest emergent level of a system exists within a range of possibility. Using some of Langer's language: in animal life, the perception of opportunities to perform instinctual acts must have some degree of freedom, a freedom that exists reciprocally with the very constraints that make the animal's existence possible. Without a different underlying theory and some kind of fundamental creativity it is difficult to even point this out. Even apparently simple behaviour is variable; LeDoux mentions that in studies in his laboratory "randomly selected rats show a wide range of conditioned freezing responses", and that the same animal "can show strong responses one day and weak responses the next" or simply variability across multiple tests. Of course we can name these *individual differences* or *fluctuations within an individual* but we have no real way of explaining them. We can only generate probabilities for this or that response, which might be accurate over time but can never tell us what will happen in any given single situation. This unpredictable edge of what actually happens points to a uniqueness in not only every existing individual organism but also every moment in time, made possible by the almost unfathomable amount of order already in the world, generated over hundreds of millions of years.

Emotion as nonconscious responding

LeDoux's detailed and empirically supported view of implicit and explicit functioning, particularly in relation to memory, enhances our understanding of the collection of detailed historical information as types of brain functioning. This information, as functioning, is necessarily unique to any given individual, within the range of possibility of the species. Placed within the overall discussion so far, it supports a fuller account of interiority. In this sense it acts as a complement to Damasio's work. In fact, LeDoux acknowledges that his work aligns with Damasio's:

> The conceptual space occupied by my own notion
> of survival circuits and global organismic states
> overlaps considerably with that of Damasio's action
> programs for emotions and drives; he and I both
> emphasise feelings as conscious manifestations of
> these nonconscious processes.[18]

However, a major difference, which LeDoux points out, is the degree to which body signals determine feelings. For Damasio body signals are the primary determinant of feelings, which means that he is much more open to animals having feelings, while for LeDoux body signals are "one of many ingredients".[19] On this LeDoux agrees with Barrett; feelings have a *cognitive component*.

> Fear and other emotions are based on assumptions, presuppositions, and expectations; they are constructed in the brain from nonemotional ingredients.[20]

As we have seen, Damasio questions the strict separation of brain and body, but he does also leave ample space for feelings that are not directly caused by current body states. His concept of the *'as if' body loop* in the brain covers situations of remembering body states without recreating them, which also generates feelings.[21] LeDoux appears to have a more compartmentalised view of the brain, and therefore sees the ingredients very much as the combination of various representations in the brain, which, again, is not the view being developed here. But it is worth noticing that LeDoux and Damasio both offer essentially hierarchical views of the relationship between nonconscious and conscious processes. Complex forms of engagement exist at a lower level than conscious experiences, which occur in the context of more elaborate (or at least more explicit) forms of consciousness, at a higher level than feelings. In a broad sense the difference between these two leading neuroscientists is that each has simply chosen a different phenomenon to label as emotion. For Damasio, emotions simply *are the nonconscious responses* and feelings occur when these become conscious, through what must be higher-level interpretive processes. For LeDoux, *emotions are the feelings*. However, citing the work of psychologist Michael Lewis, LeDoux makes the important observation (which was already suggested earlier in the discussion of Barrett's work) that children behave emotionally long before they are aware of their own feelings. This suggests that the names we learn for feeling states (and naming is key in Barrett's theory) we initially have learnt in large part through naming behaviours and situations, in which we and others are acting and interacting. It therefore makes more sense to be clear that emotion is the responding and that it can occur without any awareness of the responding as such, and that feeling is something else, another level of complexity. But these points must also be clarified by their position in terms of inner aspect/ outer aspect: emotion is the complex, nonconscious responding as seen from the outside (an outer aspect) and feeling is another emergent level from the inside (an inner aspect). Indeed, this is something that LeDoux does seem to be aware of: "Consciousness is, and probably always will be, an inner experience that is unobservable to anyone other than the experiencing organism."[22]

The clear alignment of emotion with complex yet nonconscious responding allows us to say that animals *display* emotions before we make any assumptions about an inner aspect, about what they are *feeling*. Importantly, nonconscious means that the animal (or human being for that matter) need not be conscious of the behaviour *as such*. Obviously an animal is usually awake or alert in some way when responses occur; this is why the term nonconscious is less confusing than unconscious when speaking about behaviour. Ways of understanding this level of consciousness will be discussed later. For now, we can reflect on Jonas' statement about animal life: this "precarious and exposed mode of living commits to wakefulness and effort". Both LeDoux and Damasio use terms for the simpler forms of consciousness that animal behaviour seems to require at a minimum, the wakefulness mentioned by Jonas. Naming this level seems to be relatively standard practice in theories about consciousness. But it is interesting to note the equal importance of Jonas' use of the term *effort*. Effort is difficult to think about if we see animals as complex machines that carry out complex action programs. Perhaps it borders on the projection of feeling states that LeDoux so carefully dissuades us from. But it does seem to connect with something we can *also* observe. Being alive requires this strong purpose from within the living system, a strong tendency towards remaining whole and yet resolving or absorbing situations of disharmony in whatever way is possible. Living is more on the edge than any kind of complex machine could ever be. Effort should also not be limited to the survival imperative. Exploration and interest in the world is a requirement for animals to fulfil the possibilities of their life trajectories and to create new possibilities. Attunement of all levels, both within and outside of an individual organism, creates continuity, generating enough harmony, enough balance for persisting and developing. But when we think of attunement as at least potentially creative it seems much more like effort, particularly in animals that are evolutionarily closer to us. With or without differentiated inner experiences like feelings, effort describes that a system will strive to maintain itself, which it can only do because it recognises itself as whole at some level, even without consciousness as we know it.

Emotions are appraisals

Admittedly, the suggestion that we should decisively align the term emotion with behaviour and with a level below (or constitutive of) consciousness as feeling is not straightforward or practical. We are so used to using the terms emotion and feeling somewhat interchangeably in daily life. At the same time, the ways that emotion is defined and understood in other fields does offer support for its redefinition, at least theoretically. When many researchers generate definitions of emotion, these definitions are often much more oriented towards relationships with an environment than with inner feeling experiences. One standard psychological textbook of emotions, *Understanding Emotions*, by Keith Oatley, Dacher Keltner and Jennifer Jenkins summarises a variety of definitions as follows:

one may treat emotions, at least to start with, *as multi-component responses to challenges or opportunities that are important to the individual's goals, particularly social ones.*[23]

Interestingly, the differences between evolutionary approaches to the psychology of emotion and cultural approaches, as discussed in their book, result in varying emphases on fixed species-specific action patterns and the potential for difference respectively.

Evolutionary approaches are more aligned with the concepts of action programs and physiological signatures found in the classical view of emotions (emotions as essences) while cultural approaches find emotional experience in "words, in metaphors, in concepts that permeate the conscious experience of emotions" (emotions as "discourse processes").[24] Barrett's view of emotion is more aligned with the latter.

However, all the concepts that support the view of animal behaviour presented so far—such as the *umwelts* of particular species; that relationships and communication are fundamental to nature; and that animal behaviour can be thought of as exhibiting the goals and importance inherent in the pressing forward of all life—make Oately, Keltner and Jenkins' summary definition amenable to the nonconscious actions of animals. These concepts also diminish the distance between biological and cultural explanations, as biosemiotics does. Of course, these authors do at times refer to feeling as an inner conscious state (it would be odd for a textbook about emotion to contain no reference at all to feeling states) but often somewhat distinctly from emotion and without adequately describing the relationship between the two.

Thus, Oately, Keltner and Jenkins state that "Most researchers now assume that emotions follow appraisals of an event."[25] Here their overview intersects with the work of the philosopher Martha Nussbaum, who develops a neo-Stoic view of emotions as appraisals or value judgments. Her view is based on "three salient ideas":

> the idea of *cognitive appraisal* or *evaluation*; the
> idea of *one's own flourishing* or *one's important goals
> and projects*; and the idea of the *salience of external
> objects in one's own scheme of goals*. Emotions
> typically combine these ideas with information
> about events in the world.[26]

This picks up the themes that run through our discussion of animal behaviour. If we return to the idea that complex responses to situations can be completely nonconscious and always in double relation (in that they also relate to the details of previous experience) and reiterate that perception is in itself an active responding, then the attunements of animal actions are not distinguishable from these definitions of emotion. Nussbaum uses the Stoic notion of emotion as "assent to an appearance" (which is a judgment) but expands it to "accepting the way the world seems",[27] to support her view that children and nonhuman animals also have judgment, and experience emotion. In doing so, she approaches the idea put forward here that the responding *is* the appraisal. All actions express a worldview, no matter how rudimentary. Both actions and emotions are appraisals, although we need to simplify the overall statement to *emotions are appraisals of events*. They do not *follow* appraisals; they *are* appraisals, because behaviours are appraisals. We can here return to the history of the definition of emotion, from the Latin term *ēmōtiōn-em* meaning "of action" to its association with agitation and a moving outwards. All actions adjust the individual in relation. Disturbances and fluctuations within or outside the organism are resolved or altered by the actions of the whole animal. What the animal *does* is equally an assessment of *what needs to happen*, which may be more or less accurate or successful in any given instance, but always occurs with an effort that is filled with the meaning of the situation for the animal. The seeking of best fit includes the best effort possible at the time; appraisal is always also evaluative.

An obvious criticism of this view would be that not all events and thereby not all responses and behaviours are equally important to the human being or animal engaged in them. Situations can be more or less critical and responses can vary in strength and intensity. Even if we decide that emotion is something observed in behaviour, it is unlikely we would see it in all behaviour, perhaps even most behaviour. But rather than finding ways to extend the concept of emotion to include more behaviours, which the notion of purpose inherent in the final causes that are essential to all life could justify, it is worth considering the opposite view; that the term emotion has very limited explanatory power. This is why I suggest that it is simpler and more fruitful to focus on what kind of understanding is present in behaviour and what feeling states are like and, crucially, how these two phenomena relate. They not only emerge at different levels in the hierarchy, but they are different perspectives: one from the outside, one from the inside.

10

The sense of fit

IT IS WORTH RETURNING to the foundation offered by the speculative schema and the theory of semi-autonomous systems before turning to a more detailed account of feeling. The purpose here is to remind ourselves of how human consciousness is positioned in relation to the body and the material world, so that we might also consider the possibilities for inner experiences in other organisms—albeit experiences that are potentially quite different from ours. The best way to describe consciousness is as a *being inside*, as the inner aspect of a process that exists in relation to all else or the whole of change. This only really makes sense when we decide upon it as a fundamental principle. Even so, the differentiation of processes always involves paradox, which must be taken into account. Differentiation describes existence as taking a position, necessarily in relation, and at the same time acknowledges the limits of our human ability to engage with and understand phenomena. However, once we accept these principles the concept of semi-autonomous systems as change that is partially contained, for a time, and that thereby allows for the development of a relation to its own prior functioning makes sense. The organism as a whole process unfolding over time becomes quite easy to grasp.

For the system to maintain itself, it must recognise itself as whole on some level as well as adjust itself in relation to changes at many levels both inside and outside. Behaviour occurs when the system adjusts at the level of the whole in relation to an environment. This is an outer aspect, or relation, of the process and can be observed. The consideration of complex forms of engagement, or behaviour, before turning to conscious experience preserves the orientation of speculative naturalism. Neither consciousness nor the material world is seen as the primary reality, but we note the importance of theories about the physical, natural world because we can more readily observe and discuss phenomena from the outside. Thus, the natural sciences are well accommodated within a broader set of ideas.

Understanding the categories of process/relation and inner aspect/outer aspect means that we can approach the question of feeling in a different way. I have outlined the view that complex actions do not require consciousness of them, including of so-called deliberations and decisions, or in the language offered, attunements. This view allows us to question, along with LeDoux and to an extent Barrett, whether animals experience feeling states like ours simply because they exhibit behaviours that look similar to ours. At the very least, we do not assume that they do. This point aligns with LeDoux's goal of being clear about what we are referring to when we speak about behaviour or feeling states, or discriminating between nonconscious behaviour and conscious states. However, the goal here is quite different from either LeDoux or Barrett. If we do not assume feeling states such as those often identified as emotions, such as fear and happiness, we can be *more broad* in our speculations about what animal experience might be like. This can eventually encourage us to observe our own inner experience more directly and in more detail; the concept of nonconscious behaviour applies to humans as much as animals. The question then becomes what we actually experience while we are engaged in so-called non-conscious behaviour. In turn, such observations offer further clues for a more graded emergence of types of conscious experience, in evolutionary terms, than the jump from complex actions that require only some sort of being awake to the highly differentiated inner experience made possible by so-called cognitive concepts. We need to consider what it means to be conscious at all.

Consciousness

The study of consciousness is an extensive and complicated field of scholarship. In an important sense consciousness remains one of the great mysteries of our time. While the sciences have been incredibly successful in discovering ways to understand and manipulate the physical world, they are still unable to convincingly describe this most immediate of phenomena and how it relates to the physical structures and processes we observe, not least in the brain. One point worth mentioning for those who subscribe to a materialist (or physicalist) perspective similar to LeDoux (that consciousness *is* neural processes) is that consciousness can emerge in the context of very different types of human brains. The scientist Rupert Sheldrake reports the work of neurologist John Lorber nearly forty years ago. Lorber scanned the brains of hundreds of people with hydrocephalus, a condition also known as 'water on the brain'. People with this condition have much less brain tissue and for more than sixty of the people in the study, the skull was mostly (more than 95%) filled with cerebrospinal fluid. Some of the people in this group were severely disabled, but many functioned normally with IQs in the average range. In fact,

> one young man who had an IQ of 126 and a first-
> class degree in mathematics, a student from
> Sheffield University, had 'virtually no brain'. His
> skull was lined with a thin layer of brain cells about
> a millimetre thick, and the rest of the space was
> filled with fluid. Any attempt to explain his brain in
> terms of a standard 'connectome' would be doomed
> to failure.[1]

Anomalies show us what is possible at the extreme edges. In case this example seems too extreme, when discussing the fact that children born without a cortex can still be conscious, LeDoux himself states that "much evidence has demonstrated that malfunctions of brain development can be compensated for, and when this happens, *all rules are off* in terms of what goes where in the brain."[2] However, examples such as that offered by Sheldrake seem different in degree from the relatively new discoveries about brain plasticity, even though these are very important developments in the understanding of the brain.

This difference in degree highlights the importance of understanding consciousness—or to put it more simply, experience—as the highest inner level of complexity. It does not emerge from neurons alone, even if we see neurons as dependent for their existence and development on other bodily processes. It is better described as a *perspective*. Consciousness is the inner aspect of a whole process, which is also a whole process over time, an ontogenetic trajectory. Whatever level of complexity a particular organism has reached, the emergent level of organisation that maintains the unity of the process as a whole in relation to an external environment *is* the inner aspect, and we can assume that all living processes have an inner aspect simply because they exist in this way. They need not have experience *as we know it*, but we can still imagine a position, or perspective, from the inside.

It makes sense, then, to suppose that animals more like us might be in some ways similar to us from the inner aspect; they probably have some kind of experience. Indeed, theories about consciousness are often based on where we draw the line of similarity, whether at primates, mammals, vertebrates or multicellular organisms.[3] Because of the importance of the nervous system for our human experience, a significant place *for us* to draw the line is at animals with nervous systems. However, nervous systems are evolutionarily preceded by more diffuse arrangements of neurons, as *neural nets*. If we mark this as a significant point of evolutionary emergence for an inner aspect *in principle* relatable to our human experience, then this includes most multicellular animals (in fact, all except sponges and the structurally simplest, free-living organisms, placozoa). However, the important caveat here is that we can still imagine an inner aspect for other forms of life. We cannot know whether it is *like something* to be any of these forms, although we can probably assume that it is nothing like being in the process of an individual human life. Choosing to demarcate animals with neurons is also in keeping with some important insights from biosemiotics about how change occurs, moving between analog and digital forms. Neurons may be seen as a digital form (with on/off potentials that become discrete events), while the chemicals that link neurons at synapses may be seen as an analog form (with specific molecules matching particular receptors and concentrations which reach threshold effects).[4] Thus, it is not the presence of neurons themselves that supports an increase in coordination and complexity but that the neuron offers a different kind of code at a particular level of organisation. The *switching between* codes is what matters. This relates back to a very basic principle of a system maintaining itself by recognising itself. The two kinds of code allow for a redescription that supports a new, emergent whole.

Feeling as inner sensing

Now we can finally relate all of this to the concept of feeling as inner sensing. Feeling might begin, evolutionarily speaking, with sensing the internal environment. This fits entirely with the current scientific interest in homeostasis and interoception, and its importance for the emergence of consciousness. Interestingly, Langer suggested something similar decades ago, that perhaps an animal feels the highest level of its functioning and behaviour, and that as higher levels of complexity emerge through evolution these modes of experiencing are subsumed to a feeling of the newly emergent higher level:

That somatic acts we normally do not feel were felt
in early epochs of our ancestry is certainly possible;
at some time they were the highest activities of the
archaic creatures... When the species progresses to
more elaborate functions, particularly by the
evolution of special sense organs, those new
functions arise in the context of older ones which
have settled into such perfectly habitual patterns
that they are no longer felt. The total activity of the
matrix has been raised to a higher level.[5]

Langer's view here is very similar to Damasio's presentation
of feeling as emerging from homeostasis and interoception,
particuarly in his naming of the old interior of the viscera and
the new interior of the bony skeleton, skeletal muscle and special
senses. Although it might be a simplified version of Damasio's
meaning, interoception seems to be the maps or images arising
from functions of homeostasis, from the viscera. For Damasio
these images are the "core components of *feelings*".[6] Importantly,
Damasio also describes the increase in separation of "the neural
surveillance job of interoception",[7] as found in humans, as
evolving from the more basic separation of chemical and neural
signalling; this is perfectly in keeping with some of the
foundational principles of biosemiotics. However, as discussed
in chapter three, Damasio also emphasises the *integrated
mutuality* of the various systems within the body and is critical
of the lack of attention generally paid to this wholeness. So
rather than placing feelings somehow *in the maps or images*
Langer's statement is much clearer and more accurate in the
context of the theory I am developing: *The total activity of the
matrix has been raised to a higher level.* Our perspective on this,
from the inside, is feeling; it is our experience.

Importantly here, by feeling I do not mean feeling states
usually associated with emotion, simply any kind of feeling. If we
think about it as inner sensing, feeling could be simply sensation

from inside the body, particularly earlier in evolution. But sensation seems more akin to something passively received, and therefore requires a receiver, which implies the inner separation of control that I have been at pains to avoid. We must keep in mind that feeling as it is meant here is gestalt and continuous, in the manner of experience, even though obviously for us it is also constantly changing. It is important to emphasise that new levels of coordination, required as organisms are more differentiated in their inner functioning, are emergent levels of organisation. While they exert top-down causation they are as much constituted by lower levels. Emergent organisation is simply the possibility for the continued existence of a system in its current configuration, always also in the context of a changing exterior environment. Causal influence flows both ways. But because change is largely contained in a semi-autonomous system, the highest level of organisation, from the inside, can only be of the whole. Thus, wherever in the evolutionary chain the inner aspect, as some kind of experience, becomes feeling, it must be holistic but also fluctuating within some limits; it is also a process of change.

We need to reconsider what the evolutionarily earliest forms of conscious experience might be like. As mentioned in the previous chapter, LeDoux uses the fairly well recognised term *creature consciousness* and sometimes calls it *wakefulness*. Thus, an animal can be awake and alert, capable of responding to stimuli, problem solving and acting with only this level of awareness. This state is contrasted with mental state consciousness, which includes these functions, but also awareness *of* stimuli, *of* self and *that* the self is perceiving and acting.

Thus, the distinction between these states is essentially that between awareness required to function and awareness of content. This seems like much too sharp a distinction between a kind of *pure awareness* and an *awareness of something*; indeed creature consciousness or wakefulness alone is what the term

173

nonconscious refers to. While I have aligned complex behaviour, associated with emotion, with the term nonconscious, this sharp distinction still needs to be addressed through a discussion of feeling. When we are not clear that consciousness initially occurs as feeling we can very easily treat consciousness as though it were a screen of sorts (metaphorically speaking) onto which content is then projected in later evolutionary developments, which is supported by the common and strong use of the metaphor of mental events as images. Damasio's earlier work contains a similar tension, between a pure, undifferentiated awareness, which he calls *core consciousness*, and the fact that he sees consciousness as arising as feeling—a higher level interpretation of responses, including emotions. Feeling here must be of movements and changes. Damasio's more recent work is more inclined to this second aspect of his earlier view: "we cannot discuss the physiology of consciousness without referring to feelings and vice-versa."[8]

Feeling as a sense of fit

To reiterate, behaviour, as complex forms of engagement of the whole animal with an environment, does not require consciousness of the deliberations, decisions or behaviours *as such*. All of these processes can be implicit. How then, can we characterise the emergent level of organisation such that a certain behaviour does occur? More importantly, what is this level like from the inside? So far we can suggest that it is some kind of feeling. Recall also that the organism as a whole is always seeking to harmonise levels within and in relation to its environment, or *best fit*, and that this includes trajectory and purpose, as *best effort*. The most likely experience, or inner aspect, of the adjustments that occur as whole acts but are still subject to interruptions and further attunements is a very basic *sense of fit*. Most basically, as a whole, the sense of fit, as a *holistic inner sensing*, might be a feeling of whether to continue or to adjust. For us continuity is clearly associated with general feelings of ease and okayness, while the need to adjust is associated with tension, however small, and often a sense of things being not quite right or something needing to happen. Of course, we express this in our human language, but it is worth imagining whether something like these holistic feelings occur in animals, possibly even most animals. Importantly, sense of fit describes an immanent meaning; animals might have an overall, relational sense of their situations. This last point aligns very well with the concept of *umwelt*. With a sense of fit, from the inner aspect, animals live lives that are meaningful *for them*, albeit probably in a much less differentiated way than we do as humans. Even so, life and meaning are deeply entwined, and our human possibilities for meaning arise naturally from prior evolutionary processes and forms of life.

The concept of sense of fit supports the idea that sometimes feelings of ease or tension will be more entrained with inner functioning (such as digestion or heart rate) and that sometimes they will arise more in relation to an environment, including interactions with other members of the same species. When some shift in the environmental situation is required the system might become more outwardly oriented. As explained in enactivism, the animal does not then passively receive more perceptual information, but rather shifts itself, as a whole body and whole system, into a different interaction that is either rapidly responsive or more fine-grained. In relation to the latter, the sense of greater alertness, pausing and readying might be a feeling of tension and anticipation, or simply a holistic sense of lack of fit. Another way we might imagine a sense of fit is as feelings of familiarity, which do not need to be directed toward particular objects but might simply be about whole situations, because adjustments occur in relation to whole situations. For example the migrations of birds might be possible because of their ability to sense magnetic fields (potentially from sensors in their eyes) but at the level of the whole this sense of direction must be coordinated with the whole body movements of flying. With no reflection upon direction as such, birds might experience feelings that move between familiarity and non-familiarity. Familiarity then seems like another way of saying sense of fit. We might even call it an openness to the situation or trajectory as it is. The openness occurs when things are going well.

Sense of fit can also describe the way an animal will seek out a situation of safety to restore harmony among internal physiological levels following a build-up of tension, such as during threatening situations in which actions have been blocked or suddenly altered. For vertebrates with sympathetic nervous systems, when a successful response to a critical situation has occurred, such as successfully escaping a predator by running, this might not be required. But when the activity of escape has been thwarted in some way (say, by an accident or the appearance of a second predator) some release of tension after the event might be necessary, even if the animal ultimately survived the situation. The activity by which an animal seeks and recognises the right time and place for this release is compatible with the idea that it has a relational sense of its situation. In this case, the strong sense of fit is essentially the sense of safety, actively sought out to restore internal harmony. In the right situation, an openness to this internal need or pressure is created, as the animal settling into itself, the system turning inward. Held tension is often released as shivering, shaking or completing unfinished movements of the body. The principle of releasing held charges from the body by creating a sense of safety is becoming well-established in trauma treatment in psychology and bodywork, no matter how long ago the trauma, and is partially inspired by these observations of animals.[9]

We should note that sense of fit needs to relate to any situation in which an animal's actions are well-matched to a situation, when a strong dynamic coupling occurs. Thus, this would include situations such as killing another animal for food or winning a fight for dominance with a member of the same species. In these cases, we might describe sense of fit as an openness to the edges of its ability; there is nothing essentially good or right about fit. However, in the context of the whole of nature and evolution, fit can only come about in the context of myriad ongoing relationships and attunements so there is a natural circumscribing of brutality, at least to an extent, by local and broader systems as ecological wholes. Life is made possible by both effort and constraint. Any appreciation of nature must take brutality into account while still ultimately generating an understanding of what differentiates human beings from other animals. The understanding of life that human consciousness makes possible does include the potential to attain a higher level that includes the valuing of life. Perhaps that is indeed a natural purpose of life becoming conscious of itself through evolution.

The concept of sense of fit provides for a graded evolutionary emergence of the inner aspect as a sense of self. According to the theories already presented, a self is defined by the relative containment of change, which in turn means that the system collects historical information. By definition, the history of any semi-autonomous system is present in its functioning, even if only in small ways in simpler organisms. If the inner aspect of this is indeed a kind of holistic inner sensing, a sense of fit, then it can be understood as a sense of self, no matter how rudimentary, because it exists in the double relation. This sense of self doesn't require knowing or reflecting on its own existence. The more complex memory becomes, the more discernment becomes possible, in terms of whether or not to adjust behaviour, the relation of the whole organism to its environment. This fits with the principle that greater individuation, or distance, requires more refined modes of bridging distance, or connection. We can relate this back to

Barrett's idea that the brain generates many hypotheses based on past instances and then selects the one most likely. The idea here is very similar, but does not place agency in the brain. Instead, we can acknowledge that multiple potentials exist at lower levels—seen from the outside at least partly in neuronal firing patterns, albeit always in the context of the whole body—but the creative emergence from this *is* the inner aspect, the whole process, *the sense of fit.* The experience is response and choice at the same time, always subtly shifting in degrees and allowing the possibility of adjusting the whole organism. The possibility for agency occurs at the level of the whole self and is experienced as feeling. We can assume that in simpler organisms feeling is less differentiated and more entrained with behaviour but in more complex animals sense of fit allows for greater discernment. It eventually becomes a higher level than, and a means to reflect on, behaviour because it becomes more influenced by learning and memory, albeit from the inside. Choice and agency gradually increase through evolution.

PART 4

HUMAN EXPERIENCE

11

The Biology and Culture of Interactions

MY RATHER LONG, and admittedly speculative, discussion of animal behaviour and suggestions about animal experience has been in the hope of generating a space in between the idea that animals are complex machines driven by internal programs—which makes animal experience, and thereby all forms of consciousness preceding ours, essentially irrelevant—and the notion that animals experience feelings much like ours. At heart, this is the same theoretical move again, between the two extremes of materialism and idealism, or objectivism and subjectivism.

Identifying such a space should help us to reflect more deeply on nonconscious behaviour in human beings, particularly in its evolutionary, biological continuity with all life, both animal and other forms. Not only is human meaning immanent in some very similar ways, but it arises in mutually defining, real relations with other human beings in a way that is much better described as interconnected than constructed *because immanent meaning occurs throughout nature.*

In relation to human life, the concept of sense of fit offers a way of bridging the divide between so-called biological and cultural processes, of identifying aspects of our interactions of which we are not usually aware and which yet shape our experiences, including our more differentiated feelings. Two theorists offer insights on the interleaving of biological and cultural processes: the well-known sociologist, Pierre Bourdieu (1930-2002) and the anthropologist Eliot Chapple

(1909-2000), who although much less known, could be credited as the earliest interaction analyst.[1] Their ideas can help to develop our understanding of this relational self, experienced most fundamentally through the sense of fit. While many theories exist that could no doubt also be applied here, Bourdieu and Chapple are relevant because they may both be seen as dialectical thinkers. Their work fits well with all the theories discussed so far, including the underlying process metaphysics of the speculative schema. Both are also centrally concerned with patterns of interaction, how individuals and groups are formed and constrained by broader cultural patterns, in ways in which we have only minimal, if any, awareness.

At this stage, it is also worth reminding ourselves of some of the points made about metaphor in chapter two, in particular that the development of understanding is related to repeated activities. The discussion of animal behaviour and particularly the complexity of implicit memory, only supports the idea that many, perhaps most, behaviours can be learnt, elaborated and modified without us necessarily being aware of the process of learning and modification. For human beings, many behaviours seem natural, self-evident even, as ways of being in the world and with each other. Experiences that seem natural (or as Lakoff and Johnson would say, more clear) form analog kinds of understanding that we then project to metaphorically understand other (or less clear) kinds of experience. The discussion so far, in which all life is seen in terms of levels of activity constituting and constraining other levels of activity, with the key point that life is the containment of change for a period of time, leads to the idea of the inner aspect as a holistic sense of fit. The idea of this gestalt mode of sensing, which is inherently relational, fills a gap in the theory of metaphor because it allows us to say that at its most basic, or evolutionarily earliest form, consciousness is equally an experience and an understanding. The inner aspect can only occur because the whole process exists in a stable relation both to itself and to its external environment. Even though Lakoff and Johnson mention the natural structuring of events (and Johnson later develops the concept of image schemata) eventually within theory completely aligned with these points and with speculative naturalism more broadly, a fuller account of semi-autonomous systems, biosemiotics and the emergence of consciousness helps to clarify that meaning emerges simply from the fact of being in a living process, one which must continually adjust to other processes, living and nonliving to survive and flourish.

The rhythms of interaction

Key in all this, even before language, is how we entrain to one another, or how we regulate levels both internal to the self and the interactions we are involved in. Chapple has an interesting perspective on this, and the publication of his book *The Biological Foundations of Individuality and Culture* in 1970 placed him, in some respects, ahead of his time. One of the central concepts he works with is rhythm; he initially focuses on the patterns and rhythms of the individual, strongly based in the physical body:

> From the individual cell and its metabolic processes, its synthesis of DNA and RNA, to man as the total organism, the biological rhythms are the controlling factor.[2]

At all levels, from the individual cell up to the whole organism, "some way of synchronizing or coupling all these rhythms together is clearly necessary."[3] Chapple's work is very much aligned with our discussion of behaviour and emotion, claiming that the changes in state of systems of the body (including the autonomic and skeletal muscle nervous systems, along with their chemical regulation by the various hormones) do not *produce* emotions but *are* the emotions:

> To talk about this area, one has to use awkward
> phrases like the emotional-behavioural or
> emotional-interactional or, for that matter,
> autonomic-interactional. The purpose of so doing is
> to make clear the physiological reality that overt and
> observable patterns of action and reaction are not
> mere surface phenomena, unrelated to the overall
> functioning of the organism as a biological system.[4]

The fundamental role of rhythm extends to interactions and culture; culture provides "those carrier waves which organize the biological rhythms."[5] Chapple acknowledges a key role for linguistic or semantic analysis in the understanding of culture, but he places his focus (quite unusually for his time) on *interaction investigations*. Chapple appears to see the foundation for other aspects of culture, including language, in *cultural sequences*. These are essentially the way that interactions between individuals and amongst groups come to be ordered, becoming implicit, accepted and naturalized over time.

> Each culture has a multiplicity of patterns in which
> first one person does something and one or more
> persons follow this action by another. Whether
> they be called rituals, or manners or even "standard
> operating procedures", they have in common the
> cultural sequencing of the actions and interactions
> of individuals.[6]

Children learn sequences, and in particular their timing or tempo, from the moment of birth, because babies are engaged in interactions as soon as they are born. Chapple says:

> The newly born arrives on the scene with a set of inherent
> biological rhythms, controlling much of his physiological
> and behavioural performance. As he grows older, these
> shift at different rates of speed to the circadian patterns of
> his social and climactic environment.[7]

184

Importantly, within Chapple's theory the rhythms of the individual are seen as unique; indeed Chapple extends the notion of unique rhythms all the way down to the individual cell. At the much higher level of complexity of the whole person (or newborn) the idea of unique, individual rhythms makes clear that *fitting* these rhythms to interactions in which the newborn baby is involved begins as soon as the individual enters the world. Attempting to match these rhythms could be the basis for all kinds of learning and adaptations in very early life, and for the very early sense of self as the holistic sense of fit. We can certainly say that because the newborn baby is more dynamically, causally connected with her environment, the way rhythms shift and adjust at this age sets up, to some degree, basic interactional requirements. While this will be discussed further in the next chapter, in relation to the development of feeling, it is worth mentioning that Chapple relates these requirements to temperament, defined as "observable, emotional-interactional patterns".[8] From a very early age, the ways individuals respond and react within interactions establish temperament, setting up interactional needs for life: "They are repetitive and predictable."[9] In some ways, these points might seem simply a version of *nature versus nurture* from the perspective of biological rhythms, but the point is to start to link levels of activity through dynamic concepts. This begins to highlight how timing influences us; the cultural sequencing of actions provides a means for us to attune and adjust to one another *in the right timing*. One of the most obvious activities in which we can identify rhythmic shifting is in conversation, with the timing of taking turns and pausing. While the so-called content is not irrelevant to a person's holistic sense of what is happening and how things are going, timing influences how easy or tense we feel. It forms one of the boundary conditions within which a sense of fit emerges. One only need think of how long it takes for children to learn this, to develop a stable sense of self that allows for reciprocal interactions with some degree of balance. Much of what we like in other people is based on how well our interactions match in this rhythmic sense, but because we are often focused on content, the importance of the rhythms of attentional shift often go unnoticed, even as they allow us to sense ourselves in the presence of others. Thus, Chapple distinguishes the more usual sense of compatibility, as shared interests, from complementarity: "Complementarity ignores these interests; it is limited solely to interactional synchronization."[10]

According to Chapple, we are all seeking to meet our interactional needs within our daily rhythms; we are looking for the right kind of interactions in which we can synchronise with another person. Synchronization occurs more often than we might think, but does not continue for very long, and individuals vary in their flexibility, or the range within which they are able to adjust their rhythms to another person. Given that complementarity fluctuates and is generally fleeting, we are more often than not in a state of non-complementarity, which Chapple terms dysphasia. Chapple defines this state of asynchrony as stress. Thus,

> When complementarity occurs and the
> parasympathetic becomes activated (*not* in the more
> extreme reactions), the individuals experiencing it
> try to continue its state indefinitely.[11]

Again, this perspective does resonate with some of Barrett's ideas about our continual adjusting according to anticipated energetic requirements, with these requirements redefined as rhythms. However, the similarity to Barrett's concept of the *body budget* actually highlights its deficiencies; it highlights the need to define the holistic inner sensing as an emergent level. Chapple's concepts are less reductive, but observing rhythms remains essentially a perspective from the outside; synchrony and lack of synchrony is the experiential aspect.

This demonstrates the need for a concept of holistic sensing, a sense of fit, which, once we are adults, *is* our sense of self, continually shifting as situations change, but within limits that the system recognises, presumably at many levels, including within consciousness.

Practical sense-making

Bourdieu's work offers an added dimension for conceptualising the relationship between higher-level cultural processes and individual preferences and behaviours. We can see it as a complement to Chapple's work. Where Chapple is more strongly focused on biology and the individual rhythms that are basic to interactions and thereby experience, Bourdieu is more interested in how behaviour is determined by societal structures, particularly class. He is not especially concerned with the inner experience of individuals; in fact his position on unconscious behaviour is even stronger than the one being developed here. However, he has a very interesting perspective on sense-making in practical action, which is reminiscent of our entire discussion of immanent meaning and provides a strong link to Lakoff and Johnson's work on metaphor. Bourdieu is a dialectical thinker and very much concerned with transcending oppositions between "determinism and freedom, conditioning and creativity, consciousness and the unconscious, or the individual and society."[12]

At a fundamental level, Bourdieu is concerned with the relationship between dynamic and structure, hence his work on *The Logic of Practice*. A key concept in this regard is habitus, a term used to describe behaviour as both an interpretive structure and dynamic lived experience. Habitus describes the principles by which behaviour is ordered. These are:

principles which generate and organize practices
and representations that can be objectively adapted
to their outcomes without presupposing a
conscious aiming at ends or an express mastery of
the operations necessary in order to attain them.[13]

Habitus seems a natural progression from our discussion of animal behaviour. It essentially describes the habits learnt in interactions, and, in keeping with the trajectory of a semi-autonomous system, develops early in life and is fairly robust and predictable. We identify it from the outside, but it is the structure by which we make sense of the world in our practical actions. Bourdieu describes practical belief as a state of the body rather than of the mind, and says that:

Practical sense is a quasi-bodily involvement in the
world which presupposes no representation either
of the body or of the world, still less of their
relationship. It is an immanence in the world,
through which the world imposes its immanence,
things to be done or said, which directly govern
speech and action.[14]

While it is beyond the scope of this book to discuss Bourdieu's work (which is at times conceptually dense) in detail, this idea of behaviour as sense-making can enlarge our perspective of how societal structure comes through in the behaviours of individuals and groups, that it is essentially learnt in repetitive activity and does not require conscious reflection. Through our interactions with various people and groups, we come to have a sense of what to do, which also means that we can make sense of the world. Importantly for the theory being developed here, the sense of what to do is a feeling, very much like the way I have described the sense of fit. A helpful analogy that Bourdieu uses is that of a skilled player, including phrases such as *feel for the game*, which is a way of expressing that people will anticipate plays and moves, and act appropriately. While this structure is limiting, it is a necessary condition for participation and, ultimately, experience: "nothing is simultaneously freer and more constrained than the action of a good player."[15] As we have seen in relation to the development of experience and understanding through metaphor, our experience is holistic and continuous but also has a natural structuring that we can identify, even if only after the fact. We are not aware of following a structure but we do so anyway.

Symbolic power as recognition

While Chapple sees perhaps the most important reason for seeking certain kinds of situations or interactions in terms of our attempts to find moments of synchrony with others, Bourdieu sees the actions of habitus as more strategically motivated, albeit unconsciously. Part of the reason for this is his concern with class and how class structures propagate themselves. People come to take on the habits, mannerisms and tastes of their particular social class in a way that reproduces class structure, by which the higher classes dominate everyone else. Even though class structures have certainly shifted since his major work in the late twentieth century, the concept by which Bourdieu theorises this unconscious strategizing can act as an important stepping-stone towards understanding why the sense of fit is so important. Influenced by Marxism, strategy is based on the idea of accumulating capital. However, this capital is not restricted or reducible to material wealth or economic capital. It is often termed symbolic power or cultural capital and can be described as the "degree of accumulated prestige, celebrity, consecration or honour".[16] Bourdieu sees it as "funded on cognition [connaissance] and recognition [reconnaissance]".[17]

Bourdieu is highly critical of social inequality (which is obvious in the influence of Marxism on his ideas) and tends to prioritise structure over lived experience, without paying much attention to feeling. This is evident in the degree of self-deception needed to *keep the game going*: "It is because agents never know completely what they are doing that what they do has more sense than they know."[18] We might wonder if this is too cynical a view of human life, telling us that even though they don't know it, what actually motivates people is to get what they can for themselves. At the same time, when individuals internalise social structures, it clearly does keep the game going in the service of a powerful elite. For instance, the utter desperation for recognition apparent in the explosion of social media has coincided with a serious but broadly accepted decline in economic security for many people while an elite few reap extraordinary benefit; these are two sides of the same coin, namely the belief that the individual gets what he or she deserves based on merit. Social structures do have a way of propagating themselves. They are real processes with their own inner dynamic and emergent novelty. At the same time, they are not living systems and therefore are more dynamically entrained with the activity of individuals; they are more susceptible to change, even when many individuals are involved. Thus, to persist, they must rely on some characteristic within human nature, which could well be the desire to dominate others, fuelled by the idea, or sense, that domination somehow assures security and survival. Certainly, at some level, being able to dominate others, even simply by being a member of a higher class, does relate to outcomes such as freeing a person from physical or low-paid labour and can lead to a life with more choice and greater ease. However, this kind of ease doesn't seem to be the kind of ease that is associated with a strong sense of fit, with openness and connection with others. The wealthy elite suffer from the same ills that plague so many others in contemporary Western culture: depression, anxiety, loneliness and a lack of meaning. This is not to say that material circumstances don't matter, but to invoke the increasingly well-known fact that when basic material needs are met, wellbeing doesn't increase along with wealth.

Chapple can help us look at labour from a different perspective, as a dimension of all activities and interactions. Even the point that people will attempt to synchronise with one another opens the possibility of unequal relations. Some people will be less flexible in their ability to attune, which will place others in the position of either coping with stress (or dysphasia) or attuning to the other person. Chapple's description of cultural sequencing also means that within any activity, different steps can be assigned, consciously or not, to different individuals. This "division of cultural sequences"[19] is a kind of division of labour. Chapple sees the *dominance hierarchy* as a way of ordering the requirements for activity, and particularly for the initiation of activity, as cultural sequences become more complex and groups become larger. All activities become organised in terms of who does what and when in a mundane sense, but also by creating positions for individuals in relation to one another, all of which can come to seem natural and to fix expectations—Bourdieu's *feel for the game*. In this way we exist in relation to all the positions we have been taught to occupy, particularly in early life: "The initiative and dominance variables develop early in the maturation process, and evidence from behaviour genetics indicates that they have genetic components."[20] At the same time, positions need to be available for us to take them; higher level cultural processes, to some extent, set these possibilities. Certain interactional types will be more suited to some cultures than others. The basic division between extroversion and introversion is a case in point, with contemporary Western culture offering better positions for extroverts, and thereby more social capital, including material wealth, up for grabs.

Recognition as deeper need

Being able to speak about cultural and biological processes through a single set of concepts brings out some important insights. There is no point in evolution at which meaning suddenly arises. We humans do not construct a separate world to live in, via language or any other means. The very possibility for language emerges from the interactions that emerge in relation to the types of bodies we have and the needs that arise from them, including the need for connection. We could say that all living beings have some version of a need for connection, because they must recognise the world, with its potentials and pitfalls; species can even be said to develop their own cultures, even if in a much less differentiated form. However, the particular kind of culture in which we exist at this point in history is relatively ephemeral compared to the degree of order required for humans to come into existence in the first place. This suggests that the needs met by modern Western culture with the possibilities for the accumulation of symbolic power or social capital, even if not very well, are more universally human than we realise. Such needs are more akin to Chapple's rhythmic, interactional requirements, more biologically entrained forms of connection. Yet even Chapple prioritises a dominance hierarchy. We should instead notice that domination is only one way in which humans position themselves, particularly in relation to the degree of stability generated by the desire to connect; people very often support and cooperate with one another. Cooperation, accommodation and symbiosis occur throughout nature but have been dramatically sidelined by the overarching status given to competition in Darwinian evolutionary theory.[21]

In relation to the entire theory presented so far, the need for connection could be related to the inherent insecurity of living; not only, for all individuals, the basic fact of death, but also that the selves in and by which we know life and come to experience anything are completely relational, and therefore eminently fragile and deserving of compassion. *Understanding* human beings as emergent through the nearly unimaginable, long process of evolution, in which change has become contained such that consciousness has emerged—that life can know itself—is awe-inspiring. The inner aspect of this, an *experience* of being a self, in all its joy and heartbreak, can be a similar source of wonder. The recognition of the world and the self are intimately bound. Perhaps at the deepest level of our humanness we seek not certain kinds of power or certain positions, but through those positions and the familiarity they bring we find the fundamental recognition that we exist and the world exists. We find that we are profoundly alone and not alone at the same time, individuated only in relation to our possibilities for connection. The most basic way we experience this relatedness is as feeling.

12

Infant development and differentiated feeling

I HAVE CHOSEN to use the term *sense of fit* to convey that consciousness arises initially as the inner aspect of whole acts carried out in relation to situations. It encompasses the idea of holistic, inner sensing that is different from the special senses and more active and integrated than the passive reception of information from inside the body. It is ever present and often subtle, because even when we are strongly focused on a particular activity or single aspect of a situation, we still have a more general, holistic sense of how things are going. I made some suggestions as to what that feeling might be like in other animals (shifting degrees of openness, familiarity, ease or capability) but more to provoke a reflection upon or sensing of these feelings than to name animal feelings specifically. Openness, for example, might feel like a combination of ease, safety and outward orientation, whereas capability might involve a little more effort and striving, a kind of brightness. Unfamiliarity can feel like an unsteadiness or diminishing in some way. The subtlety and relatively amorphous nature of these kinds of feelings is reminiscent of the philosopher Eugene Gendlin's concept of the felt sense: "that unclear edge in the border zone between conscious and unconscious."[1] They are more holistic and relational than sensations but less defined than the feelings we usually associate with emotion.

Gendlin's work, developed in the late twentieth century, is relevant here because, as both a phenomenologist and a psychotherapist, he points to aspects of our experience in a way that is highly original as well as developed in therapeutic practice. The felt sense is very similar in some ways to the sense of fit, particularly because the felt sense is both a holistic experience and a relation to complexity: "A felt sense is the wholistic, implicit bodily sense of a complex situation."[2] Gendlin is also very clear that the felt sense is different from emotion. Emotions are stronger experiences, more easily categorised and usually similar across instances; each time I feel angry, my experience of anger is more or less the same, even if the circumstances that make me angry are different. The felt sense, on the other hand, is always unique and changing as situations themselves are; it is simply the overall, inner sense of a situation. However, the idea of sense of fit, particularly in the context of animal experience and the evolution of consciousness, makes the distinction between emotion and feeling stronger by seeing emotion more clearly as action. Gendlin also acknowledges the expressive nature of emotion, which supports this stronger alignment with action. This is particularly evident in relation to catharsis, when a person might have a good feeling while expressing what are usually understood as unpleasant emotions:

> Catharsis feels very different to the person
> experiencing it than to the person observing it. The
> inexperienced observer feels it as being bad. This is
> because the waves of emotional intensity are
> coming at the observer. Anger and pain coming
> toward oneself do not feel good. But for the client,
> when those same waves of energy roll outward
> from the inside, they feel very good.[3]

The emotion and the feeling are clearly different in this particular situation. The emotion is the action that serves to adjust inner levels in relation to the situation; it releases pent up tension. The good feeling that can go along with this is not only of the release of tension but also the fact that the situation has allowed it; the person must feel safe enough to do it. Thus, the most basic sense the person has of the situation might be of safety and ease, then a pressure that is followed by an openness to the act once it has started, to follow it through to its end. Importantly, catharsis is no longer seen as unambiguously of therapeutic benefit; Gendlin explains that catharsis lends itself to repetition more than resolution, and current trauma treatment discourages it. But we can see catharsis as one end of the spectrum of the difference between emotion and feeling that is always present. We adjust in relation, and often display emotion while feeling something different. Much more needs to be said about this last point, because obviously we sometimes name feelings without engaging in actions to adjust them; I can be angry while doing nothing. But still, if we observe our experience a little more closely, we might find that our anger can be many different experiences, from an *impulse* to shout or use force, which is more like an assessment of a situation to a *feeling* of bursting with heat or pressure, which is more attuned to the inner aspect of the anger that wants expression. The difference between these and the role of language in unfolding the process of experience will be discussed in the following chapter, but will make more sense following a discussion of the development of differentiated feeling in early childhood, in relation to the work of the philosopher Martha Nussbaum.

Early life experience

One way of entering into a deeper understanding of feeling is to imagine the experience of newborn babies and young infants, experience that is without language and without a fully formed sense of self. Such speculation can also support us to observe more directly how our own, adult experience actually is. Usually, we cannot directly remember our very early experiences (because few, if any, explicit memories are formed before about three years of age) but still some of our present experiences might resemble it in some form. We can also infer experience by observing the expressions of infants, particularly in their interactions with caregivers. Approaching the development of feeling in this way is a mainstay of some fields of psychology, particularly psychoanalysis, and numerous theories explore the development of relationships and attachments in early life, and how these extend into adult life.

Yet before discussing feeling in more detail it is worth highlighting that the strong emphasis on early experiences that is present in psychoanalytic approaches to development aligns very well with the overall way we have understood semi-autonomous systems. In the early stages of any living system, the highest inner level of functioning is much more dynamically engaged with the external, environmental conditions than later in the life of the system. We are more entrained with and therefore highly influenced by whatever happens. The boundaries of the system are actively created as it moves through the early developmental stages, within a range set in place by the process of evolution. For human beings, much has already happened before birth, in terms of active genetic expression in dynamic engagement with cellular and higher level developmental processes, as well as an important degree of individuation from an environment. But at birth the infant becomes dependent on interactions to meet all their biologically based needs. This sudden increase in distance requires a whole new set of dynamic expressions and interactions that profoundly shape the entire life of the system. Possible trajectories narrow as actual interactions happen. A history begins to form, to which the system will continually relate in later stages, in keeping with the double relation. The importance and continuing relevance of early experiences cannot be overemphasised, and is characteristic of living systems generally.

Nussbaum's book *Upheavals of Thought* has already been mentioned in our earlier discussion of emotion; her concept of emotions as appraisals supported the theory being developed. In line with the current discussion, Nussbaum also sees emotions as heavily influenced by past experience, particularly in childhood:

> I shall argue... that in a deep sense all human
> emotions are in part about the past, and bear the
> traces of a history that is at once commonly human,
> socially constructed and idiosyncratic.[4]

Nussbaum outlines a theory of infant development that is influenced by modern psychoanalytic theory but also draws upon the Roman philosopher Lucretius (99-55 BC) to differentiate itself from these contemporary theories. Both approaches are organised around the infant's complete dependence upon others to meet all its biological needs. Infants *experience* this dependence as "a felt need for the removal of painful or invasive stimuli, and for the restoration of a blissful or undisturbed condition."[5] Thus, our initial experience of life, as feeling, is the movement between fairly extreme states, with the gradually dawning perception that caregivers or *restorative agencies* are present in the world to regulate these states. However, initially the newborn will not perceive the restoration of calmness or ease as performed by a distinct object. Rather, she simply exists completely within a kind of transformational process. Such ongoing and tumultuous change means that *the world itself* is "felt from the start as chancy, porous, full of uncertainly and danger."[6]

This early experience gives rise to the second facet of infant neediness, "a need for comfort and reassurance that is not reducible to its basic bodily needs."[7]

Nussbaum differentiates her work from early psychoanalytic accounts of infant development, which tend to see all needs in terms of bodily gratification, on the basis of this second need, which appears to be inspired by Lucretius' "account of the nurse, who both feeds and calms it with soothing words and caresses."[8]

While we cannot ultimately know the inner experience of an infant, it seems reasonable to identify comfort and reassurance as a distinct need. The theory of the development of semi-autonomous systems, along with the speculative schema, reinforces this. While physical needs must be met to guarantee the development of the self as a *material* system, this cannot describe the system as a whole. To persist, it must have some way of identifying itself as whole over time. Sensing itself as whole from the inside, as experience, arises in relation to the developing infant's differentiating feelings, which are also the most basic sense of self. As the boundaries of the self begin to form through these shifts and changes in experience, the restoration of ease plays a crucial role in the system's sense of its own wholeness, the stability of experience. Even if *physical* experiences assist in the restoration of ease, such as the experience of being held and touched, the need for comfort describes more than this. It is a relational need for the development and persistence of a stable sense of self and world.

The way changing feelings are mediated by external sources of comfort and reassurance supports not only the eventual development of boundaries but also gestalt perceptions of the relations between the self and the world that inherently involve beliefs about causes. We might imagine that very early feeling experiences are simply of change happening, alternating between ease and distress. Perhaps the implicit memories formed at this very early stage are simply based on repetitive experiences of *when this occurs, then this occurs*, related to the duration of certain feelings and levels of distress, the timing of changes. These are holistic experiences that include emerging perceptions of the world and the self and the way things tend to happen. As the world and the self differentiate, these early feelings are a dynamic sense of fit, as the self is forming, that we can imagine moving between ease as a kind of openness or buoyancy and tension as a kind of resistance or withdrawal.

Nussbaum describes these very early experiences using more traditional terms for emotion:

> The earliest emotions are likely to be fear and
> anxiety, when the transformation is temporarily
> withheld, joy when it is present, and increasingly, as
> time goes on, a kind of hope for its blissful arrival.[9]

I have tried to describe early feelings more as the sense of a relation to a situation, which can be clarified by once again aligning emotion with action. It is very difficult to imagine infant experience with terms such as fear and joy, but it is quite fruitful to observe their behaviours in these terms. One of the reasons for this is the high level of activity of infants, again fitting with the high degree of physical entropy at this early stage. Emotions such as joy are displayed in wanting to interact, contact, explore and play, or even by facial expressions and vigorous arm and leg movements in babies. Feelings of openness, delight and safety might accompany this. While these experiences are unambiguously good in the same way that joy is, the distinction remains important. Similarly fear can be observed in reaching desperately for a caregiver or turning away from something, perhaps experienced as urgent withdrawal, or in extreme cases possibly quietness and stillness, with a feeling of dread. Anxiety might be witnessed as fussing or changeability and experienced as an amorphous uncertainty or unsteadiness. Imagining feeling in this way reinforces the very basic notion that whatever we feel is an emergent level of an orientation towards the world, one which extends throughout the animal kingdom and perhaps even beyond, of moving towards the beneficial and away from the harmful.

Making the point that infants are also always engaged in action to adjust, even if those are fairly limited early on, also emphasises the importance of an infant's perceptions of the self and world as inherently causal. At a very early age, the infant is more dependent upon action as display or expression, because babies literally cannot move themselves around and must attract the attention of caregivers by other means. Activities such as crying and screaming, then, have an actual, causal effect but the mode by which they adjust the situation is largely dependent upon others (although the action by itself will also release tension; for instance even crying that is not responded to will eventually abate). The very early perceptions of transformations between various states from which a sense of fit and early sense of self emerges are also perceptions of causal relationships. They are not simply perceptions about other people but about the world much more generally; the self and world reciprocally map each other. Nussbaum explains this in terms of emotions: "Fear and joy and love and even anger demarcate the world, and at the same time map the self in the world."[10] She sees the connection with action, because she understands emotions also as recognitions of "the boundaries of its own secure control".[11] The self, then, is formed by repetitive experiences that are inherently involved with one's ability to have an effect. The boundaries that form through reciprocal exchange and interaction do not initially form as an infant's perception of itself and other people but of its position in, and relation to, the world much more generally. This explains why very early trauma can mean that a person's most basic experience of not only relationships but the world itself, experienced as feeling, can persist through an entire life in which the world is perceived as profoundly unsafe and unfriendly and can be tied up with the debilitating perception that there is nothing one can do about it, thus feelings of despair and hopelessness. Because the self emerges initially *as* these feelings, and any further discernments that language later makes possible can only emerge from the range provided from these, it can be nearly impossible for a person with such trauma to even think about themselves and the world in other ways.

The ambivalence crisis

The cornerstone of Nussbaum's theory of infant development is influenced by Lucretius' description of "the infant's central perception of itself... as an entity very weak and very powerless toward things of the greatest importance".[12] Nussbaum describes the development of emotion in early childhood through the *ambivalence crisis*, which outlines the development of feeling consciousness such that love and anger come to be directed at the same object. This crisis begins with the gradual awareness of the restorative agencies as outside oneself, present as a rudimentary form of gratitude that gradually becomes love when one's needs are met, and as anger when needs are not met. Importantly though, in very early life the sense of inside and outside the self is vague and unformed, and therefore these emotions might also be directed toward parts of the self or simply cause confusion. If we imagine the feeling states of these emotions, gratitude and love might be an openness that expands and is close to merging, a complete ease perhaps, and anger the opposite, an extreme narrowing of experience, a feeling of blocked helplessness. These are also inherently causal perceptions, related to the changing perception of the infant's own role in changing states. Thus the infant wavers between the positioning of omnipotence, "in which the entire world revolves around its wants"[13] and helplessness, the realisation not only that the world does not exist entirely to satisfy its needs but also that the satisfaction of needs is entirely outside its control.

> All omnipotence is coupled with helplessness.
> When an infant realises that it is dependent upon
> others, we can therefore expect a primitive and
> rudimentary emotion of shame to ensue.[14]

The ambivalence crisis occurs when boundaries are formed enough that the child recognises that love and anger are directed at the same object; the *impulse* to strike out against or hurt someone she also loves, *with all the vulnerability that need brings,* gives rise to the pain of guilt. The way that the young child will handle the feeing of guilt depends on the way that, through birth and infancy, they have come to experience the dynamics of interaction that eventually bring about this crisis. These dynamics have formed perceptions of the self as much as perceptions of others and the world, specifically the child's degree of acceptance of their own neediness and imperfection. A parental holding that allows omnipotence and neediness, by providing "suitably responsive and stable care"[15] will allow for the creation of a relationship of trust that defines the way the child both perceives itself and interacts with the world. Thus, the resolution of this crisis brings about an appreciation of difference that supports the child in her ability to engage with and explore the world and human relationships:

> a good development will allow the gradual relaxing
> of omnipotence in favour of trust, as the infant
> learns not to be ashamed of neediness and to take a
> positive delight in the playful and creative, "subtle
> interplay" of two imperfect beings.[16]

The way we come to perceive and experience our own separateness relates directly to the quality of our exploration of the world, the pleasure we come to take in difference; it can be a source of delight as well as a source of pain. The inner experience of difference, through the development of feeling, drives individuation. The paradox of freedom and determinism that is central to the development of living systems, which the speculative schema makes sense of at a foundational level, is clearly relevant here. Limits create both potential and restriction, and the balance of these—order and disorder—is required to optimise the development of the self. Life emerges from all kinds of subtle interchange *at all levels,* and, with the emergence of consciousness as feeling, it can be experienced.

In the context of Nussbaum's theory we can see how

important the rhythmic fluctuations described by Chapple are, phases of synchrony and asynchrony that must relate to the overall health and stability of the system as it moves through developmental stages. We can also suggest that the particular rhythms of an individual at birth, the beginnings of temperament, might be more or less suited to its caregivers and its unique and changing situation. The point is not to attain perfectly synchronised interactions but for interactions to be within a range of harmony and disharmony that supports development. As individuation continues and a sense of self develops, the young child must contend with both her experience of the world and her experience of herself. Thus, Nussbaum suggests that if a history of interactions has supported her well enough "the child comes up with the ideas of justice and reparation". Guilt can be assuaged by atonement; "the very badness itself can be made a source of good."[17] However, if the child has not been able to accept its own imperfection then the emotion of shame is more likely. While guilt is potentially creative, shame is nullifying. Nussbaum is here worth quoting at length:

> From this point on, the child agrees to live in a
> world in which others make legitimate demands
> and one's own desires have appropriate boundaries.
> If one oversteps those boundaries, one must pay a
> penalty; and insofar as one forms aggressive wishes
> toward others, one must struggle to limit the
> damage those wishes do, and repay the objects of
> aggression by creative and benevolent efforts. But
> because those moral demands rescue the child from
> helplessness and depression, they are at the same
> time welcome demands. Moral guilt is so much
> better than shame, because it can be atoned for, it
> does not sully the entirety of one's being. It is a
> dignified emotion compatible with optimism about

one's own prospects. The structure of morality thus performs a "holding" function for the child, giving her a feeling of safety. In this sheltering structure, she can play and exert herself.[18]

Already, at a young age, the history of the self, the interactions through which boundaries have been formed, plays a large role in whether an experience of badness will become guilt or shame. The main difference seems to be whether the self is stable enough to find a path out of the badness (reparation) or whether the badness will permeate the whole self. Guilt and shame seem like a difference in degree than altogether different experiences. The *feeling* of shame, a badness that overwhelms or dissolves the sense of self, shuts down the creative potential of consciousness while guilt does not; the desire to connect becomes channelled in atonement. That shame dampens the natural, living process in this way emphasises how extreme an experience it is, particularly for a young child.

Nussbaum emphasises the role of early development but also leaves room for a major role for broader social structures and institutions than the immediate family or caregivers. However, her narrative of development, especially in the context of the broader theory of nature, highlights that human feeling develops within somewhat predictable ranges. This provides the basis for thinking about human morality as based on principles that permeate nature; certain conditions encourage the flourishing of individual life forms within the interconnectedness that makes them possible. This offers support for Nussbaum's claim that the possibility of reparation in the organisation of human life and society at any level will be more effective for everyone, and that shaming practices will generally be ineffective.

Unique habitus

Nussbaum's view of development also helps us to build on Bourdieu's work. Bourdieu's concept of habitus is very useful because it names the dispositions towards situations that organise actions and perceptions in their entirety. It is a way of thinking about a set of structures, which are implicitly learnt, simply through living, that mean that people understand situations and express that understanding in action in particular ways. The attempts to adjust that become patterned through interaction are the most basic kind of habitus. These are highly dependent upon repetitive, individual experiences—each person develops their own habitus—and they give rise to the experience of both the self and the world, which emerges most fundamentally in experience as feeling. Thus, the ways that interactions and feelings tend to repeat in early life can determine much about a person's ongoing experience. This idea has much in common with some psychoanalytic views, such as those of John Bowlby, who proposes that the models we form of ourselves and relationships through early attachments can affect many other relationships through an individual's life, particularly intimate and other significant relationships.[19] For instance, if someone receives too little response and attention in infancy, he might become reticent or anxious in many interactions through life. If someone receives too much attention she may become self-centred and domineering in many interactions. Or, depending on the individuals involved, these circumstances might result in the opposite outcome; ignored individuals might become dominating or, if attention has been controlling, overly supervised individuals might fail to develop independence and become anxious. The important point here is that habitus is deeply relevant to a person; maintaining certain styles of interactions keeps the self and the world stable. If we acknowledge that this occurs at the fundamental level of an emergent sense of self, then we can understand why it can be difficult for people to change their styles when they are not working for some reason. The need for the sense of self to survive is as strong as that we usually think of as a purely biological imperative for survival. This point reinforces again the idea of the strength of the need for recognition, which may be as fundamental as the recognition that we exist and the world exists, and confirmation that they are connected by stable relations.

The process of inner differentiation, experienced initially as the feeling of separation, that makes individuation possible is a tenuous and difficult process to navigate. It requires strong boundaries and structures to be established very early on. Development through the ambivalence crisis shapes our very basic sense of our own power; this is a deeper and more individualised version of Bourdieu's symbolic power. This basic sense of ourselves continues in habitus, elaborated in the interactions by which individuals learn ever more detailed actions, as a set of fundamental beliefs about how we might affect and be affected by the world. The need for secure and reliable beliefs at this level establishes the fundamental possibility of the experience of being human. Developing a sense of self allows for experiences of separation and connection. We must mediate the possibilities that arise from this by seeking to fit as best we can in the world as much of the time as possible. The manner by which we come to sense ourselves and to know the world through all our mutual adjusting can be understood as a set of *beliefs* because we learn patterns of adjustment from particular interactions and circumstances that *could have been different*.

Furthermore, even the quality of physical exploration of the world—which infants and small children engage in nearly constantly during their waking hours and learn complex action sequences as a result—is heavily influenced by feeling that is more than the physical, material body. It includes a sense of self that must be highly influenced by an overall sense of fit and safety established in early relating. Even at an early age, the way a child explores will be within a range of potential as it also elaborates those inborn aspects of temperament. Thus, the child's developing sense of fit in the world is very much guided by feeling. One quite straightforward example can be seen in the gendered experience of the body and its physical limits. The ways in which infants and young children are encouraged to use their own bodies are dynamically influenced by the perceptions of caregivers and other adults as to how safe they are and what they can physically handle. For instance, adults often engage in more rough and tumble play with boys than with girls, although this may be changing somewhat in many societies. Nonetheless, boundaries provided will play a major role in determining how the child *actually* explores the physical world, which will in turn have a huge influence on his or her sense of her own body and physical capability through the whole of life.

Of course, these examples are not particularly ground breaking and they are also quite general. However, in the context of the theory developed through this book, the notion of the implicit structures of habitus, formed through interactions and formative of experience, becomes both more nuanced and more a part of nature. We can see ourselves as formed of patterned interactions in the same way as other living systems, and perhaps other natural processes. That change, as cause of itself, is fundamentally creative rescues us from a completely deterministic view of early life experiences that are continually present. The leading edge of emergent experience is always creative, even if based on the heavily patterned processes of implicit memory, as well as the evolutionary range of possibility for human experience. Implicit memory, which responds to ever more details in situations, emphasises the uniqueness of each individual because the details of individual history are always utterly and necessarily unique.

Even so, in actual life we can feel weighed down by the past and often our feelings are at odds with other ways of understanding a situation. We might be attracted to partners we know are not good for us, say things we know we don't mean or become disproportionately upset by apparently small events. If we reflect on things, we might know that we do certain things repetitively but feel unable to change our pattern. Or when we do make efforts to change behaviour or the way we see things, we might feel completely undone, not ourselves or, even worse, unwittingly find ourselves in similar circumstances again despite our best efforts. Yet this is where a view of action as appraisal and feeling as a higher level understanding of a situation can come into its own, because we can not only reflect on our own behaviour, we can learn to see the past in the present. Of course, the context of language and explicit memory must also be included, a consideration of the process by which consciousness develops with these. The key in this is learning to appreciate that the depth at which relations we engage in and observe is real. They are an outer aspect of the process each of us is in, the inner aspect. The remainder of this book will elaborate on these points.

13

Unique, individual metaphors

THE PURPOSE OF redescribing habitus in relation to early development in the previous chapter, along with positing a certain kind of recognition as a fundamental need for the development and experience of a self, was to emphasise the uniqueness in our histories at a finely detailed level. Our histories are literally present in our experience in a way that is not simple to explain.

Here it is worth mentioning again the paradox that underlies experience: it is dynamic and continuous but also structured in ways we can identify. Through previous chapters, I have outlined a theory that does not hide from this paradox but centralises it as foundational to anything we can know or experience, even as it relates also to the unfathomable wholeness of change, which we cannot directly know or experience.

Nonetheless, we can quite easily identify repetition in almost any of our own actions, particularly the more mundane activities of everyday life; this is not where the difficulty lies. For instance, as adults, we can notice the centrality of repetition when we intentionally and directly engage in explicit learning. We simply repeat the activity until some kind of threshold is crossed and much less effort and focus is required to carry out the activity; we have gained a skill. From this, we can infer that learning generally occurs through repetition, even when we are not aware of the process, as is especially the case in early childhood. Such experience and inference does support the idea that we create a circuit or strengthen a neural pathway for that particular activity; the complex but potentially discoverable processes of implicit memory make sense here. But even so, how the structure is recreated in the present, by a whole, living body in relation to changing circumstances, requires more explanation.

The natural structure that any process takes has been described with the fairly simple concept of the act, a discernible arc of movement or change in relation. We can suggest that even biochemical processes at the micro level follow this basic form.

This allows us to say that even if we can identify a lower level neural process that corresponds to certain kinds of behaviour, we need not think of that neural connectivity as a kind of step-by-step instruction to the whole behaviour that emerges. It may be a whole act in itself, but we can also identify a separate wholeness in the actual act of behaviour; the neural pathway or combination only becomes a structure from the perspective of the whole, living body, which moves and acts.

The new level of activity that this gives rise to is a different, emergent, whole act. The creativity of this particular level lies precisely in its adapting to the particular environment for the whole act *this time* it occurs.

This perspective helps to centralise those processes of tinkering mentioned by Barrett. Multiple possibilities are present at the level of neurons and we can assume that this is the case all the time. But we cannot meaningfully speak about a perception or action being *chosen* by a separate entity (the brain) as though once the choice is made an action is engaged like a software program. The act is not the same each time even if the general structure is there; in fact it can never be exactly the same because all situations are in principle unique. Acts, and the implicit memories of them, are always being elaborated upon in new situations, even if that elaboration is at times a straightforward strengthening of the pattern at the lower level.

The recognition of whole situations

Once again, I have entered into a discussion of feeling through a discussion of behaviour, because behaviour is more easily observed and because so much of our behaviour occurs without our direct awareness of it. Rather, our awareness is, early in life at least, of feeling, specifically the sense of fit. Even though later in life it is possible to go through our days with very little focus on feeling, the sense of fit is still there. In this regard, what may be observed or inferred at a lower level as tinkering is—as a whole, emergent level—the sense of fit as a feeling that may be more or less comfortable, tense, safe, certain etc. As explained in previous chapters, the sense of fit develops into sense of self. We naturally learn to harmonise not only with outside situations but with our sense of self, our history of feeling—a double relation that exists but cannot literally be separated out from experience.

Undoubtedly, the ongoing creative emergence of experience requires that lower levels do exhibit more (or at least enough) habitual functioning or order to support the degree of disorder from which any new level emerges; creativity requires possibility. So, at the same time, we can acknowledge that a high degree of repetition probably occurs at the level of implicit memory, albeit in relation to constantly changing circumstances. As was outlined, if rather briefly, in the previous chapter, these patterns of memory form at least partly in relation to repetitive interactions with caregivers and increasingly with others as a life unfolds. An understanding of self and world is created over time, which is also an experience of self and world. This early sense of fit develops a sense of self, an overall way of being in the world and being able to respond in ways that other people understand and help to calibrate, and which continues the process of elaboration. Thus, we must deeply question the notion that the brain predicts situations and then instructs the body accordingly; the natural structure of adjustments to situations is holistic. Having a sense of a whole act that fits a situation is not the same as prediction. The wholeness *includes* how the situation will play out. It may be true that certain phases of acting contain more possibility for adjustments than others; perhaps, once an act emerges from an impulse, a narrowing of possibility exists at the lower level. Even so, we feel our way through situations as we continue to recognise them.

The goal of briefly going over these points about implicit memory here is to open up the difference between repetitive memories, or simply functioning, at this lower level and the instantiation of identifiable structure as experience emerges at the level of the whole body in present time. Some of the processes that we equate to the recognition of situations at a nonconscious level (implicit memories) can certainly be seen as categorisation. This seems to be how Barrett sees them. But memories at this level, or just functioning, can also be elaborated in many complex ways.

For instance, when we have been harmed in some way, a characteristic of the situation in which this occurred can become associated with harm even if no causal relationship existed at the time. This is the experiential co-occurrence mentioned by Lakoff and Johnson that provides the foundation for projection into new situations. Such contextual conditioning, even if complex, is quite straightforward to imagine in relation to perceived physical threats in the world.

Yet it is more difficult to imagine in relation to maintaining the sense of self, which is also necessary for survival. We tend not to think of stable experience as equally necessary for survival as physical safety. Different individuals may also be assumed to vary more in how they maintain stable experience.

To think about what actually occurs when we recognise any situation, we should remind ourselves of the difference, described in earlier chapters, between categorisation and metaphor, keeping in mind that they are best seen as a continuum. The work of Lakoff and Johnson, and later work by Johnson, powerfully demonstrates how metaphor shapes our understanding of phenomena.

However, metaphor is also said to shape our *experience* of phenomena. This claim is more difficult to explain, because it is very difficult to explain those apparently more clear or more basic experiences that we then project onto other phenomena, without positing an absolute foundation for experience. Johnson explains these more basic experiences with the concept of image schema, gestalt forms of understanding and experience that simply emerge through repetitive activities and form the basis for further projections. But recall that explanation of these was heavily focused on physical interactions with objects. Such a focus downplays the purpose and effort that makes individual lives meaningful, even in animal life, and only accounts for feeling in its kinaesthetic, body-based manifestation.

We have already seen that metaphors at the level of language cannot be completely arbitrary. Certain metaphors work because of similarities in the phenomenon being projected to the phenomenon being understood via metaphor. Those similarities might be co-occurrence, a quite simple happening at the same time, or a more nebulous experiential similarity. I discussed the example of *a relationship is a journey*; here we can say that both journeys and relationships have a characteristic unfolding over time that is similar enough for different people for the metaphor to hold. The metaphor then organises the way we not only *conceptualise* but *experience* relationships.

For instance the idea that a relationship has some kind of a *direction* may not apply to many relationships, but the way we understand relationships via the journey metaphor might lead us to expect that a relationship *should* have a direction and then act accordingly, such as by ending a relationship that doesn't seem to be *going anywhere*. Certainly, many relationships go through some predictable stages, but not all and not for everyone. Thus, the metaphor might hold at the cultural level and within language but not be equally useful for all people or in all situations.

That some experiences are *more clear* might simply be a case of them being *more common*. The way we move our bodies through space on a journey and experience the sense, or feeling, of setting out, moving or travelling, and arriving may simply be more similar amongst different people than experiences of relationships. This idea fits entirely with the notion that the details of individual histories of relationships are both more different and more strongly anchored in implicit memory because they have formed the self at a fundamental level. For instance, it is relatively common for young children to become jealous of one another, even if experiencing love for and connection with each other at the same time. But jealousy—the result of either interactional needs not being met or the fear that they will not be met—can mean that very young children will compete and vie for attention. This can cause genuine disconnection in family relationships. Depending on a multitude of interactional and general life factors, particularly for parents and other caregivers, this situation can be handled in different ways with different outcomes for each person. For a newborn baby, the competition of an older sibling might fracture and interrupt the very interactions by which the sense of self is forming, while for the older sibling, at a different stage of development, interactions might be fractured in a different way, perhaps shock at the sudden change or a sense of loss. Interactional patterns might be set up for the whole family that persist or even strengthen over time, which parents might find irritating or even distressing, and require more time and energy to manage than is available. Thus, for the children in this scenario, one metaphor that more aptly describes relationships might be *a relationship is a competition*; interactions must be sought after and struggled for, and the meeting of interactional needs might be perceived as directly taking something from someone else. Importantly though, the positioning of each child within this sense of *a relationship is a competition* is different and depends on a multitude of intricate factors specific to the rhythms and interactions of this particular family. There is nothing inherently wrong in the situation. These kinds of scenarios are simply the complexity of life occurring. They are what we must navigate as humans and particularly as highly individuated beings, and given that creative possibility exists in all experience, a number of different outcomes are possible. But for *these* individuals, the concept that *a relationship is a competition* is never explicitly known. It is simply the way that the understanding and experience of relationships co-arises through repetitive situations. Each individual is positioned in a certain way, within the structure of these situations, and develops a sense of self that includes this positioning. Each person feels a certain way as a result. Thus, someone might feel insecure or even vaguely guilty in any close relationship and have not much idea why. At the same time, these feelings or the situations that occasion them probably feel familiar, in a way that may be either disconcerting or not even noticed. Certainly, some of these early life patterns can be discovered; this is very often the content of psychotherapies. But that a present-time feeling is both real and present while highly representative of past experience is surprisingly difficult to grasp, probably more so when tied up with the sense of self at a basic level.

Feeling as a metaphorical process

The point of explaining such a scenario in the context of the understanding of metaphor is that it allows us to make some important statements about feeling. If implicit memory (which is a precondition for us understanding anything) is a relation to past experience, but below consciousness, the feeling that emerges at the level of the whole body is necessarily interpretive of this in relation to present circumstances. Feeling is both present and past. But we cannot separate present and past out from experience, because it is gestalt and continuous. Feeling is our immediate experience and understanding. However because we rely so heavily on our past experiences *while we also* creatively interpret them in the present *and continually* elaborate and enlarge the contexts for particular interpretations, the arising of feeling is a metaphorical process. While an unusual statement, this is not surprising in the context of biosemiotics. Metaphor is not a function of language specifically; it is a natural process of change that we can observe quite easily in language. Something stands in *for* something else *for* someone and experience emerges in a way that is both highly structured and profoundly creative.

If feeling is a metaphorical process, in which the projection of one kind of situation organises the understanding and experience of another kind of situation, then we should reconsider the idea of fundamental physical experience in light of the development of a self. For instance, we can think again about the development of image schemata for *force*. Johnson's explanation is based primarily on repetitive, kinaesthetic experiences. Thus, our development of various concepts of force, such as compulsion, attraction and enablement, is based on experiences of moving the body in space in encounters with physical objects. This seems fairly straightforward when we think of the way children play with toys, enjoying their efforts while simultaneously observing the outcomes of their actions. However, the *feeling of* and *for* various forces, the experience of them while they are occurring, which eventually generates implicit structures or concepts, is more than of the body in space. It includes an emerging sense of self, which is heavily based on prior interactions. These might be physical but they are also, perhaps overwhelmingly, interactional. Compulsion, enablement and attraction are also *feelings*. They emerge in interactions, particularly as caregivers' responses organise the behaviours—and thereby to a large extent the experiences—of young children. These feelings are also perceptions of causal relationships, particularly very early in life. The feelings of our own actions as we improve in our ability to use and move our bodies are already organised in some sense by how we perceive ourselves; the child who has been responded to well enough will have a much stronger sense of herself as able than the neglected child, who might even experience the world in general as thwarting or disempowering. This is not to say that our bodies and the way we move them do not play a central role in our learning and forming concepts, but rather that these are *dimensions* of our experience, separable only in principle or in hindsight. Even if we are absent-minded or engaged in something technical that requires a focus on the physical, we never act for no reason. There is overall *purpose* in our physical efforts; the fullness of feeling, even as a very basic understanding as sense of fit, can take this into account.

Aside from the broad account of infant development in the previous chapter, I have so far spoken very little about particular, differentiated feelings that we can name. This has been to establish clearly that individuals have somewhat consistent experiences before these experiences are further organised by language. These experiences arise as a self develops through repetitive relations and interactions. Because implicit memory can be strong and highly contextual as well as more strongly weighted in early life, before language is learnt and explicit memories are formed, these consistent experiences are highly individualised. Thus, even though particular, differentiated feelings most likely occur within a human, physiological range, the situations that occasion them can be infinitely varied. They are as much based on an individual's position in a situation as on physiology, both of which are outer aspects of the experience itself, ways we might observe the relation or structure from the outside. The situations that occasion particular kinds of feeling in an individual are as definitive of the process as any actual, physical feeling because the occurrence in relation is at the heart of the formation of the self. Feeling as a sense of fit, and later as differentiated feelings we can name but also as vague and changing senses of the inner body all exist within the continuous gestalt of experience. Feelings are modes of understanding as well as experiencing situations. They are more generalised than the way we further develop understanding via language, but they are also, in their relational aspect, highly structured and detailed; in this way they align with Johnson's conception of image schemata.

Unique, individual metaphors

Describing feeling in the way I have, particularly in the context of the concept of metaphor, clarifies that while we all exist in a human *umwelt*, we also exist within a unique, individual *umwelt*. My feeling is an interpretation in relation that depends on the fine details of interactions I engage in and have already engaged in, always from a very specific perspective. That perspective is formed through repetitive ways I have taken up positions in situations throughout my life, but also the ways others have positioned me in situations, right from birth, quite possibly even prior to birth. Positions are ways we can describe the structure of situations, and they are actively created by higher-level cultural processes and by group and family dynamics. We entrain to each other to maintain stable relations so that we can also maintain stable relations within ourselves, formed through our histories. Given that the dynamics present in early life are so formative of later experience and that, in Western culture at this time, we tend to live in small family groups, our feeling experiences and our ongoing positioning in situations are enormously influenced by family dynamics and early attachments. At the same time, the degree of dependence of all babies and young children on their caregivers means that it is fair to assume that all human beings go through some version of the ambivalence crisis.

This crisis sets up feeling experience within human ranges of openness and connection, and withdrawal and disconnection, as well as fundamental ways of maintaining the sense of self in the face of difficulties, all of which is highly dependent on our resilience to difference and separation and our delight in the subtle interplay occasioned by these very perceptions.

However, human ranges can only occur in relation to specific situations, and cultures will no doubt have different themes depending on the way things are done and how relationships are handled. But that implicit memory responds to details in situations, which may be more or less causal or relevant, means that experience is individualised within cultures. This might mean that some individuals will have more similar experiences based on their positioning within their families than within their culture. In Bourdieu's terms, our *feel for the game* includes how situations play out as we also participate in them, helping them to play out. This is often easier to observe in more dramatic and emotional situations; we enable each other, even when we are not aware of it, which is usually simply a familiarity with our own positions, ways we personally deal with positions of intimacy or authority, or even with mundane social interactions. Attempts to synchronise with others are always happening and highly dependent upon repeating what has worked before and avoiding what has not worked. Our attempts also rely on positioning and perceptions about causes in the past, even if causal roles were originally misperceived, as is often the case in children who feel responsible for situations they cannot possibly control. As a fairly mundane but common example, some people are more accommodating than others and try to minimise friction in social and personal situations, perhaps the result of growing up around dominating people or conflict in the family. This might work well in highly charged situations but be less useful in stable or neutral situations. If a person is sensitised to conflict they might engage in more accommodating behaviour than is necessary, by listening, agreeing etc., which could be frustrating or boring for another person who wants to engage or be challenged. Alternately, such behaviour may be sensed by a third person as an opportunity to dominate or be self-aggrandising. If individuals recognise themselves then the situation continues. Perhaps the second person's feeling of boredom engages previous experiences of disinterest from significant people or caregivers, so although *this* person may not enjoy the encounter she also knows herself here. She experiences some combination of frustration or loss and familiarity. The self-aggrandising person might drone on about herself and feel quite alive and energised, but perhaps with an underlying or unknown shakiness born of a previously unmet need for attention. And these particular positions could be engaged by each separate individual in response to quite specific cues in a situation. Nonetheless people sense which positions are available and either take them up or disengage from the situation. The situation itself partially dictates the possibilities; between two overly accommodating people nothing will happen while, conversely, most situations cannot cater for more than one person who needs to be the centre of attention. Whatever happens between human beings is genuinely happening. Positions and interactions order not only social relations but relations to physical circumstances and the natural world, in much the same way as animal behaviour.

Of course, our human interactions can become much more finely ordered by communication with language, but because we are often not aware of what we are doing, this also needn't be the case. As LeDoux describes, we often use language to describe and justify what we are doing, even when we don't really know why. At the same time we can all observe, to an extent, our own actions and those of others and agree on terms for various feelings that we infer. Take the example of courage. People who are less sensitive or more robust in their feeling experiences or simply more strongly positioned in relation to risk-taking might behave in ways that indicate courage. A strong person goes out to fight a fire. Another person stands up to harassment. One person jumps into a river to save another. Situations that occasion courage involve perceived danger of some sort, committed actions and unknown outcomes. Children might develop courage by sitting still through a dental examination or interacting with a dog they previously feared, but they will probably learn about courage as much from watching what others do and from stories about brave actions. The odd part, which is easy to miss, is that the person whose actions appear courageous might be feeling something different. The robust person's courage might be more adrenaline-fuelled and exciting than someone else's.

Alternately, sometimes people feel that their own awards to recognise courage are not warranted because they didn't feel anything, they only acted, with what we can now term a strong sense of fit, of the right action for the situation. Of course, we can still define this as an act of bravery, defined from the outside, in the behaviour. At the same time, a very timid person might need a great deal of courage simply going about her daily life. Perhaps *this* person has a familiar feeling of anticipating a situation with trepidation, gathering internal resources and moving forward into the unknown, perhaps a feeling state that combines reticence and dread with openness and purpose. If a particularly empathic observer points out that this timid person is courageous, she might realise or notice more *that particular feeling* she often has but has never thought of before as courage. While naming, in this situation, can certainly bring experience forward, the *feeling* of courage is already there in the characteristic relation to the situation *for this person*. The inner aspect or feeling of courage could well be quite similar in different people but we cannot get at it because we cannot generate artificial situations to make people feel the same thing.

As suggested many times now, feelings arise in a whole, living body in present time but this process in itself is always in double relation to past and present. This point helps us to go beyond the division between the classical view of emotion and the theory of emotions as concepts put forward by Barrett, a move which, at a fundamental level, generates a new position beyond the divisions of mental and material, idealism and materialism. Thus we can identify elements of both views but then create a synthesis. Using the term feeling instead of emotion (which this book has hopefully already justified well enough) I suggest that feeling has a stable relation to what happens at lower levels physiologically and at levels outside the body, in circumstances and interactions. There is potentially a *high degree of repetitive structuring*. However, I also suggest that the processes that generate feeling are similar in form to those that generate what we normally think of as concepts, a point that aligns strongly with Barrett. With the notion of metaphor we can synthesise these two points. The theory of metaphor and the extensive research that supports it describes how concepts form and are used in language and culture; they are consistent and agreed upon at this level. Within individual experience through an ontogenetic trajectory, consistency occurs more at the level of the development of a self, the ongoing creation of experience, which relies on memory as it also generates and further elaborates memory. Our feelings are a relation to our repetitive adjustments to situations, similar to categorical prototypes. However, they may be highly influenced, *as memory is,* by prior perceptions that shift them and by singular events, such as events that are either very meaningful or traumatic. They are also *creative adjustments* in the moment. The strong weight of our histories is certainly limiting but it provides the very possibility for our uniqueness, for the high degree of individuation possible in human beings, which on some level we can see as change becoming conscious of itself.

The profoundly creative process by which this happens can be summarised by describing a self as a set of unique, individual metaphors. The idea of these unique, individual metaphors preserves the stability necessary for any living system to persist over time, without positing an absolute foundation for experience *and* without descending into the relativism that dissociates us from meaning and value. This perspective has many repercussions for the way we view human beings and their relatedness not only to each other but to all of nature.

14

The creativity of consciousness

DESCRIBING FEELING with the concept of unique, individual metaphors is a way of understanding individuation and experience, but on its own cannot thoroughly describe the activities of consciousness. Understanding how feeling arises does not in itself explain the actively directed processes that we traditionally associate with the mind, such as focusing attention, thinking and language-based communication. The theory of metaphor already explains a great deal about how abstract concepts are formed, which may then be used in the everyday activities of speaking and writing, and in the more specialised activities of planning, formulating arguments and making theories. From the perspective of the theory of metaphor discussed in this book, feeling as unique, individual metaphors offers a fuller account of the generation of image schemata, as highly structured but individualised modes of experiencing and understanding situations from particular perspectives. They are strongly established early in life but also continually elaborated and creatively engaged in situations. Alternately, from the perspective of the broad theory of nature presented through this book, metaphor is itself simply an example of a natural process, an inherently creative form of change whereby fluctuation within stable limits makes new interpretations and thereby new forms possible. Still, it is important to explain how the more actively directed processes of consciousness, particularly those involving language, interact with feeling in the development of experience moment-to-moment. This is clearly an extensive topic. My intention is therefore to make some suggestions about principles of functioning based on the theory developed in this book, which help us to reflect on feeling.

Language allows us to make much finer discriminations in the world and in our experience and then to elaborate upon these, both within ourselves, in our internal processes, and in interactions with other people with all the ways we use language to communicate. Learning language provides a means for the development of an apparently highly specialised and separate activity within experience, which can be completely internal, such as when we think, plan, consider, ponder or ruminate. But ways we do this can be more or less involved with feeling. At times feeling might seem a dynamic aspect of such an internal process and at times more separate from it; for instance planning the agenda for a meeting seems more directed and separate than ruminating about a difficult relationship, which can seem much more passive and pushed along by feeling. However, the point here is to retain the focus on the gestalt, holistic nature of experience, as throughout this book, and to see any conscious activity as always within such a gestalt; this is in alignment with the enactivist perspective. Even the most abstract, language-based activities, such as writing a theory, always occur in relation to feeling and to action, as the expression of effort and purpose in relation to a situation, and the inner aspect of this.

Within experience, language helps us to separate out holistic forms and to then use summary forms or shorthand versions and project them in all sorts of ways. The theory of metaphor details this process. But even if language is more generally agreed upon, the underlying schema that allow it to form and develop needn't be seen as in principle different from other gestalts we learn and remember implicitly, including how certain situations usually play out, from our particular perspective. However, a difference remains: experience is individualised while language must be collectively agreed upon. Even if language can then further organise experience, the basis for it—our sense or feeling of our relation to phenomena—is highly individualised. Thus, in an important sense, language bridges the distance created by individuation, even as the process of individuation continues. Moreover, language further supports this process but can also undermine it. How language interacts with feeling is a key factor here, and very important for development.

Separation within holistic experience

Given that the theory outlined through this book centralises hierarchical organisation within systems and that in some situations we can identify active thinking processes as quite separate from feeling, it is tempting to think of such activity as a *higher level* of processing. For instance, in his earlier work, Damasio details a hierarchical view of consciousness, organised around four levels—basic life regulation; the nonconscious responses he identifies with emotion; the emergent level of feeling; and the higher level of extended consciousness, which includes explicit processes such as autobiographical memories, recalled knowledge, planning and reasoning.[1] Outlining consciousness as hierarchically ordered in this way supports Damasio's important claim that feeling is integral to and necessary for the development of so-called higher forms of consciousness and that feeling is always present; it is the basis for our sense of the meaning of anything. In more recent work, Damasio strengthens this stance, emphasising once again the role of feeling in the perception of meaning. While these are useful divisions, it is also worth considering consciousness more holistically and how variations occur within the ongoing gestalt of experience. The question then becomes less concerned with the notion of a *higher level* and more interested in *separation within* a whole process as part of the ongoing development of that holistic process.

Gendlin's concept of the felt sense helps here; feeling is an ever-present aspect of conscious experience that guides its further development. For instance, we have a felt sense of a whole situation which pushes our description of it forward. We can only name what is happening or some other aspect of a situation because we already have a sense of it, even if sometimes only at the borders of our awareness. In this view, what appears to be an active and directed process (such as speaking to another person) actually moves between active and receptive modes. We feel into what comes next, and if we are unsure we pause and feel into the edges of our experience. We engage the sense of fit here as we gauge whether what we say next fits with our sense of what it might or should be. Gendlin has described this at length in relation to the process of counselling; the pausing and feeling into is termed focusing.[2] Much of his view is in fact based on observation of the therapeutic process, notably that some people will engage in focusing much more naturally than others and that therapy tends to be more successful for these people; change happens for them. Others need to learn this, how to feel into their experience. Focusing is a way of bringing the implicit into awareness but Gendlin is careful to point out that the implicit, that which is at the edges of our awareness, that we feel into, is not literally there, fully formed, under the surface. "Feeling responds to present living; it is not a hidden package underneath."[3] Such a view supports the perspective developed in this book, that experience emerges creatively at the level of the whole person or organism; it is not a direct effect or translation of some lower level neural pattern, even if we can discern repetitive structure there. Similarly, experience is not a direct effect of an external situation, even if the structure of that situation from one perspective recreates our history, by its similar structure to that we have already experienced.

Gendlin points out that our felt sense of experience, say, as we reflect on situations in our life or in our history, requires precise terms to carry it forward. This supports the idea of a high degree of structuring in situations and the memories of them that is particular and precise even if it does not literally exist fully formed in our heads or elsewhere. The process of reflecting and carrying forward fundamentally relies on the feeling of recognition, which is basically the sense of fit; we can see our experience is a process of separating and then integrating, or alternately splitting and becoming whole. Indeed, we can identify the principles of change described by biosemiotics here. When we see language as operating within a whole process—the continuous gestalt of felt experience—then we can begin to understand why consciousness is so creative; it switches between analog and digital forms. Language (a digital form) selects from an already existing continuous process (an analog form) thereby carrying it forward in a paradigmatic process of creative change. This point clarifies the role of naming within experience. The experience is already there but naming brings a particular aspect of it into focus, which shifts experience within limits rather than constructing it from very general ingredients. Importantly, this gestalt of experience is only possible because specific and structured relations actually occur at levels below and above, in double relation to past and present.

Myelination: significance as discrete forms in relation

It is worth reflecting on what we really mean by the digital form here. Concepts and words demarcate a holistic form of our experience well enough that they can then be joined together in larger wholes, substituted amongst one another, compared to each other and used creatively. But at least some, perhaps most, of these holistic forms emerge simply through repetitive activity prior to language. The embodied approach to cognition might say that these forms are of the body doing something; they are kinesthetic or sensory-motor activities we come to remember and recognise, and eventually learn names for. I have suggested that they are more inclusive of the perspective of the developing self, a more holistic version of the *feeling for* any activity that includes purpose and individual perspective. The *feeling for* allows us to act and interact without continuously attending to the situation or the act itself. This holistic form must be remembered, or at least re-engaged in some way and the present feeling is interpretive of *this time* it occurs. But of course when we use language and concepts we do not engage the feeling for every single word, because we are moving along in whatever situation we are in (although we can do this if we need to, where there is ambiguity) and because sentences create new wholes that relate to and move our experience along. Words and sentences then, demarcate a summary form that can stand in relation to continuous experience, even if that continuous experience is a reflecting within ourselves. They generate the sense of something as they also stand in for more detailed experiences. Many cognitive scientists would use the term *representation* here, but this term encourages us to imagine an entity that is stored somewhere; I am avoiding it to create space to think of the digital form in a different way. It is helpful instead to view the digital form as discrete *in relation to* continuous experience. In essence, then, the question is how holistic experience becomes discrete in relation to itself.

Hierarchy theory and biosemiotics provide the background theory for suggesting an answer to this question by considering time frames. Thus, the summary forms of experiences that become amenable to naming, which may have provided the possibility for human language to develop, might be simply faster versions of the same processes. Potentially, the same lower level process, or a version of it, is recreated, albeit more quickly than if we are actually carrying out an activity or learning something. I am referring to neurological processes here, including relations to the body that might be termed maps, with the important point being that the neural process simply becomes faster in relation to the timeframe of ongoing conscious experience. This is very much like the way Barrett describes intrinsic brain activity, except it should be seen as *a relation* to experience that can only generate a sense of it; the process in itself is too fast to recreate experience, which would have to be a state of the whole system in action. The processes of learning and remembering have been much researched and described in neuroscience from the physiological perspective of the growth and development of neurons and their synaptic connections, thus essentially describing the creation of circuits and pathways.[4] However, research into the physiological process of myelination is beginning to suggest that this process may also be central to learning and adapting through the life span.[5] Myelination is essentially the insulation of neurons (usually wrapped in a spiral fashion with gaps or internodes) such that conductivity is improved. Electrical signals travel around ten times faster through myelinated compared to unmyelinated neurons. The process of myelination is somewhat different in the central and peripheral nervous systems and is carried out by different cells, but the principle of insulation and enhanced conductivity remains very similar. Imagining the process of myelination fits well with our actual experience. After much repetition, certain patterns of signals are suddenly faster. In our experience we suddenly know the entire sequence of something at once; *it becomes discrete in relation to our ongoing experience.*

Perhaps the most interesting aspect of this process of insulation, and the most innovative, is that it allows for separation within an already existing and developing whole system. Such separation can be interpreted in terms of the scalar hierarchy: one of the fundamental principles of the functioning of hierarchical systems is that faster processes constitute and are constrained by slower processes. Faster processes usually constitute lower levels in the hierarchy and the higher up the hierarchy the slower the process; for instance, the movement of the whole body is slower than the action potential of a neuron.

The ability of a hierarchical system to actively reinforce processes within itself and make them faster (ie. by insulating particular neurons) to a certain extent steps outside of the conventions of how processes are organised into whole systems in a way that optimises ongoing stability. This means that *the system can create another description of itself*. We might say that in human beings with language, feeling is one description at the level of the whole in relation to circumstances, and our conscious, explicit descriptions using language are another. However, the descriptions of language cannot be a description of the whole because the processes underlying language can be somewhat separate within the nervous system; the entire system is only indirectly constrained by them. Perhaps it is clearer to say that we *can* think somewhat independently of our bodies, albeit with concepts we must initially learn through our bodies, but this activity nonetheless occurs within our ongoing, actual situation; and feeling is always available as an ongoing, actual sense of things, even if very subtle. This brings out the point that while language does provide for more detailed descriptions of situations, these descriptions can be less accurate in their relation to the self than feeling, which can only develop in relation to detailed, individual history. Another way of saying this is that feeling cannot lie, whereas with language we can say anything. At the same time, feeling can be so individualised, particularly in terms of the circumstances in which it arises and in its more extreme manifestations, that it can be difficult to see that it is actually a form of understanding. At times our feelings do not appear to make sense; at such times we construct other explanations for them, accept the explanations of others or do our best to simply disregard them, hoping they will go away.

Enhanced conductivity through the process of myelination (insulating particular patterns) might be related to assigning importance to particular interpretations of situations over others. It is thought to have arisen in animal life for rapid threat detection and response.[6] Greater efficiency increases speed and means that certain protective behaviours become more likely in certain situations. Again, we should be careful not to assume that the conduction of signals through particular patterns of neurons directly causes behaviour or that myelination *is* the process of assigning importance; we are only inferring from the outside here. The behaviour is an interpretation of a situation, both perception and response, and certain neural patterns may increase the probability of a behaviour in the context of the ongoing state of the whole, living body. However, the faster responses through myelinated neurons might provide the physiological possibility for overriding other, slower responses. This fits with the fact that responses to threats most often involve movement and that it is the nerves associated with motor responses rather than internal functioning of organs and systems which are myelinated. As Damasio also points out, myelination functions as separation within a system that helps the system to protect itself, but the system must nonetheless also form an integrated whole.

Language can minimise feeling

If myelination works by the principle that an increase in speed and efficiency is a way of assigning significance, then we can imagine why this physiological capability paved the way for language. Language is a way of rapidly assigning significance, and can be externalised in a similar way to behaviour; using language is a behaviour in the same way that thinking is an activity. In the context of the maintenance of stable experience as imperative for survival, language is very important because it bridges the distance between people, the distance of the individuation from which feeling experiences arise.

Much of child development occurs as a result of bridging this distance with language. Adults and others constantly offer explanations and give instructions that, ideally, help children to organise their behaviour and manage their own feeling experiences. These can be extreme early in life but must gradually become organised such that children can participate in collective life, eventually as adults.

However, we have already seen that explicit explanations are necessarily offered within the limits of already existing patterned interactions and the feelings these occasion from particular perspectives. Such interactions are already more or less attuned to the rhythmic needs of the individual within the maintenance of stable group relations such as within a family. Even so, language seems to have an overriding potential. This potential is obvious in relation to behaviour (adults can tell children to behave differently) but less obvious in relation to the way it organises the perception of positioning and inner experience. Adults can explain situations to children in all sorts of ways that contradict their feelings. This might help to stabilise their feelings, particularly in scenarios that are more benign than the child's experience of it; a broken toy can be fixed, a disagreement can be worked out, a mistake can be apologized for. However, in other scenarios, particularly those involved with attachments to caregivers, explanations can force a child to choose, albeit not consciously, between their own experience and what others are telling them. As discussed in earlier chapters, a system naturally seeks best fit, as wholeness within itself and in harmony with surrounding circumstances. If feelings are strong but there is no possibility of adjusting them by expressing them in behaviour, as emotion, then best fit must be sought in other ways and language offers one way to do this. For instance, children might make excuses for abusive caregivers or decide that they deserve abuse as a way of reconciling their complete dependence and their need to fit in a situation. But because explicit explanations do not constrain the system as a whole, then these explanations will only be partially successful. Feeling and the lower level ongoing impulses to behaviour will need to be accommodated or absorbed by the system in some way, such as by physical restrictions or holding patterns in the body, or by an overall functioning that becomes adapted to high levels of stress hormones. Interestingly, the protective function of the motor system of the human body mentioned by Damasio, supported by the process of myelination, might carry over into language; explicit explanations often fulfil a protective function because they keep feelings (which are other, more generalised explanations) at bay.

If an infant or young child experiences too much asynchrony (from repetitive misattunements or misunderstandings all the way through to neglect and trauma) then explicit forms, including particular behaviours, might come to dominate in a way that minimises feeling. A sense of self will still develop based on a sense of fit but probably with much less feeling. Over time this means that the whole process of conscious experience, and the sense of self, develops within much narrower limits and therefore less creatively. The child, young adult and eventually adult will rely more and more on unrelated explicit explanations for feelings when they do arise and for nonconscious behaviours that continue because of their history in protecting the self. Such responses are initially based on excellent survival strategies for the creation of stable enough experience, but become less and less adapted to present situations. For some people it can become difficult or almost impossible to attune to and therefore connect with others. This is particularly true when early experience has included too much shame; the self must constantly evade the perception of its inherent badness. The behaviours to avoid this, and the threat of dissolution that it brings, will continue to *feel right* in some way even as more and more contradictory information is collected. Thus, people do things that end up the same way even as they wish to change and they feel less and less, in the most extreme cases holding onto positions that have never served them but nonetheless have, unhappily, helped to create their individual *umwelt*.

These points bring us to one of the trickiest aspects of feeling, which in the context of the theory presented seems much more of a riddle or conceptual challenge than the relation between the so-called mind and body, which has been largely overcome by the speculative schema and the theories that followed. The fact that explicit forms of memory and language can reflect on inner experience as though they are separate from it is paradoxical; these discrete forms are both separate and not separate at the same time. Experience depends on feeling; without feeling, language would have no meaning. But we can also use language to indirectly alter our experience and to create new explanations separate from our present feelings in a situation. Thus, the two forms present in experience (analog and digital) that make consciousness so creative can also create great disconnection among people. For instance, people can run on and on with the only feeling, the only sense driving them, a belief that they are right, and with only a very basic sense of fit that lacks nuance and is likely to be heavily biased. Such situations are where the efficiency of the sense of fit (that we can perform many mundane activities without reflecting on them) becomes problematic. This is especially the case in a world that values speed and efficiency above all else; people in Western societies are not encouraged to attend to their feelings, explore options, take time or even to really listen to one another. When we do not consciously attend to feeling, particularly as part of the process of engaging with others, we are more likely to rely solely on those summary forms that barely engage the actual body, if at all. This is known in psychotherapy as dissociation.[7] It has a strongly protective function that literally keeps people alive during extremely stressful situations but is much less helpful in ordinary life.

Noticing feeling in relation

At the same time, the opposite situation—that we attend only to our feelings and take them as unbiased assessments of situations—can be equally problematic. Feelings position us in a way that is inherently tied up with beliefs about causes. If we fail to understand the deeply historical and personal nature of feeling then we tend to believe that the present situation is the sole cause of whatever we are feeling, when its causal relationship is actually the instantiation of an existing pattern that can vary enormously in intensity or even in causal cues that were originally unrelated but are nonetheless implicitly remembered. Feeling is a matter of projection, in the same way as metaphor, but based on personal experience. Therefore, feeling can be more or less appropriate to the present situation. The only way we can discover how well it actually fits is to consciously work with it in what must be at once quite rational and deliberative process—reflect within ourselves, recognise our own patterns, talk to others—but must maintain, at the very least, a subtle focus on feeling and how it changes with our suggestions. We discover more in ourselves when we relate creatively to situations by observing thoughts and feelings and shifting explanations among possibilities to observe how we then change; we find what has been there implicitly and has now creatively arisen.

Granted, when things go along well enough in daily life, we might not need to examine our feelings and consider our positioning. At the same time, life is full of difficult and uncomfortable situations that we must navigate as best we can; we might wish to work with feeling when we become aware of unpleasant experiences and positions. Understanding our positioning can also help us to try out new responses. For instance if I know I have strong reactions to authority figures because they remind me of being dominated within my family then I can be a little less involved with the feeling of being thwarted. I can then see more clearly how *this situation* is and whether it requires my letting go or taking a firmer stance in regard to some issue with *this* authority figure. So many of these kinds of situations exist along with the potential that we hold them more lightly and that the feelings pass more quickly, or when they do not pass or we find them equally strong that we can experience conviction in a calmer way, as we continue to observe our position with curiosity rather than righteousness.

Even though language and outward observation play important roles in altering our experience, the notion that we can change our feelings solely by changing the way we think about things fundamentally misunderstands the nature of human beings. We are vulnerable and self-protective beings who fear dissolution in much the same way as we fear death. But we also have the potential to choose and to change, to find new ways of relating to each other and the world that grow from our existing experience, including our flaws and idiosyncracies, rather than denying them.

When we are able to engage creatively with our own experience, we naturally shift a certain way. Greater openness towards situations emerges and more space within limits becomes naturally available; we can find new edges of our experience and our engagements with others. We can experience greater compassion for ourselves and show more concern for others, because difference can be met with less resistance, giving way to the subtle interplay that naturally results when we acknowledge our own imperfections and accept those of others. To some extent we can transcend the paradox of experience, that it is both made possible and limited by strongly patterned memories and situations. We can be more subtly who we are and engage with others with greater wisdom and presence.

CONCLUSION

To return to the title of this book, *taking heart* encourages us to understand and accept that feeling is unique and important; this in itself is an act of kindness towards ourselves. *Making sense* acknowledges that feeling is always an understanding; it is meaningful and reasonable in a way we can discover even when our experience seems inappropriate, exaggerated or just plain wrong. Within a broader social perspective, *making sense* suggests that we can find a way of understanding the position of human life in relation to nature, defined as all the processes and relations that form the world as we know it, which can help us to connect our situated knowledge of the world with our sense of meaning and value. Thus, the project of understanding human feeling within a theory of nature (in this case speculative naturalism) addresses the inward, personal nature of our experience but also recognises the fundamental relatedness of experience, with each other and all else. This provides the background for beginning to understand causal connections, our positioning in relation to all kinds of processes; to the manifold intricate, interwoven interactions, of stabilities that take form and change. While the goal of this book has been to develop a theory of feeling, this goal implies a broader social intention, that we might collectively take heart in relation to the monumental, existential issues humanity currently faces and the changes we must make. These are fundamentally issues of our own survival and flourishing, and our dependence upon stable and thriving natural systems and environments.

In terms of human experience, I have tried to describe just how much of our behaviour is automatic and nonconscious and that this is simply a part of being human, a kind of prerequisite for all the things we are able to do and to experience. I have also tried to put forward a clear and convincing argument about the need for stable experience; it is a matter of survival. This idea of stable experience makes an important link to those processes that already transcend divisions of body and brain —homeostasis and interoception—while preserving feeling as a holistic, emergent, and therefore creative level, one that each of us is uniquely within. Seeing this connection to, but separateness from, lower level physiological processes can in turn help us to understand how working from within our experience is not separate from the whole, living, physiological body, as human beings have long discovered in the healing potential of practices such as body-focused meditations, dance and movement, and even supporting and consoling each other with physical contact.

Even so, human beings go to great lengths, consciously and unconsciously, to avoid their own feeling experiences. Again, this can be vital for the maintenance of stable experience, always in the context of maintaining consistent relations with other people; we need to view this aspect of our humanness with compassion and understanding. At the deepest level, stable experience reassures us that we exist and that the world is as we believe it to be. While it is straightforward to understand why people become afraid and avoid situations that might result in physical harm or death, it is less obvious that many human behaviours aim to avoid experiences that might bring overwhelming feeling experiences, even temporary dissolution of the sense of self. Shame is perhaps the paradigmatic experience here, although phobias are another example, and the most extreme manifestation might be psychosis. Even more obscure is the fact that people often maintain painful, ambivalent or even destructive positions to maintain stability, which is not an indictment of human nature, but evidence of the strong coupling required for a self to emerge, of the protectiveness of consciousness in relation to difficult and overwhelming feelings such as despair and hopelessness, as well as shame and fear.

Yet understanding that present feeling so strongly bears the mark of the past means that we can become more open and curious towards our own experience, when we feel safe enough to do so. Here is where the physical body and experience are most obviously perspectives on the one process, of the self over time. When feeling is allowed into conscious experience (when we do not endlessly adjust ourselves and situations to avoid it) we become able to notice the natural direction of the system as a whole, from the inside, as feeling, towards internal resolutions that bring about openness, acceptance and compassion, those experiences that we must value, nurture and work towards as the evolutionary possibility present in the experience of being human. These tendencies, if supported and practiced, offer us a way to face the difficulties of life, the pain of loss and death, and to openly witness the staggering, wondrous reality that we are even here. This in no way suggests that opening to our suffering or facing our losses, our mistakes, or our flaws is easy. This opening must be encouraged and cultivated and requires courage, persistence and strength.

Understanding feeling in the way I have described it through this book does not mean that we should only attend to feeling, even if in quiet moments this is a valuable strategy. Rather, understanding feeling as emerging from lower level processes in the context of higher level processes—this *between* character of feeling—means that we give more space to feeling *as* we also observe what we are doing, including what we are thinking and what is going on around us.

This *levels* approach, thoroughly justified by hierarchy theory, is somewhat evident in burgeoning therapies such as dialectical behavioural therapy, which bridges cognitive behavioural therapy and mindfulness-based techniques. It includes exploration and acceptance of feeling but also efforts towards cognitive and behavioural change, while acknowledging the role of safety through the therapeutic relationship. Thus, the strategy of observing and accepting feeling is central, but the levels of action and explicit understanding, as well as interactional levels, in relationships, are all addressed.

When we see experience in relation to the highly entrained yet always somewhat tenuous physiological stability of which it is the inner aspect, in the context of the nearly unfathomable degree of order developed through millions of years of evolution, the necessity for stable experience seems more obvious. So much change is contained within the human being as a semi-autonomous system that our ideas about how we might change our experience, the highest, inner emergent level of complexity, become more modest and incremental but no less profound. When we work with the way things actually are, understanding the processes of the natural world from which we emerge and of which we are a part, we can approach the notion of changing our experience with much more patience and forbearance. When we let go of the idea that we should quickly transform our experience into something wholly different—to feel constantly happy, to never suffer, to recover spontaneously from an illness—then we open up to a different kind of change, developing subtlety within our own feeling experience and the physical and physiological changes this can bring. We might then experience moments of sublime attunement in our meetings with the world: sudden empathy for a stranger, delight playing with a child, a breathtaking silent encounter with a wild creature, or simply love for those who have unintentionally hurt us. Such moments do not make us immune to other realities of our human history—aggression, greed, humiliation, mistrust—but we become more flexible and resilient in our own experience. We can hold these realities differently.

The term *unique, individual metaphors* is meant to convey the *betweenness* of all our realities, our individual and collective experiences. Interactions at all levels—from the most simple encounters of a transaction with a shopkeeper, cooking dinner with a friend, or even saying goodnight to a loved one, to the more large scale and complicated of a government considering recommendations and passing legislation, the recovery of a community from a natural disaster, the emergence of the zeitgeist of a particular time—are formed of and in turn form stable, repeating processes that have identifiable structures. They exist and are actual but the ways we know and participate in them are from our own perspectives. Whatever we feel is, along with our history, a genuine understanding of and response to that which is actually occurring, albeit at a more generalised level than the more precise characterisations of language. As we participate in processes we also create them, but we only have a sense of how to create them because we have done or seen something similar before. If the most fundamental yet unfathomable reality is change that is cause of itself, and the most basic way that we can characterise anything from our human perspective is as processes formed in relation (knowable from the inside as experience and from the outside as any relation we identify) then when we change from within, when we pause or wait or completely stop our adjustments in behaviour and language and observe our experience such that we, in time, change our patterns, we effect *actual* change, however small in relation to the cosmos, or significant in relation to someone with whom we regularly interact. We form a different relation to that person, or group or even higher level social process. We literally make new positions for all other processes, even if those positions are not taken up or do not come to fruition. While the view I have developed in this book is in many respects similar to some forms of psychotherapy, on this point it is very different, as a result of the underlying metaphysical foundation. The *extension* of this metaphysical orientation requires a great deal more explanation than is possible here, but we can generally state that for interactions to arise requires people to have a relation to the situation that fits the relations of others, even if those relations are very different.

And while this view must be explored with extreme care and sensitivity, it does create a space for observing the events and interactions around oneself as occurring in relation, although certainly not a simple causal relation that makes us *responsible* for what happens to us.

The embedded relatedness of the self as a process over time, in principle to all else, also means that we can at least *consider* less usual feeling experiences, including those that people often attribute to the rather nebulous term *spiritual*. While most of us are highly contained (in that we are influenced by our past experience such that creativity happens in small increments) creating more inner harmony over time, which brings the self into more present relations, potentially means that we can extend our perception of relatedness through our feeling experience. Here we would not then contact *other* realities but simply *subtler* realities, for instance a subtle sense of living or being that relates us to all forms of life. This is, after all, our ancient history and is in an important sense actually within each of us, literally in our functioning.

Of course in everyday human life our reflections on feeling tend to be much more mundane. Feeling obviously emerges from *all* the processes we can observe from the outside. These include physiological rhythms and entrainments going on in and outside of the body, arising as cycles of hunger, tiredness, desire and aging, and whatever habits we engage and challenges and stressors we regularly experience. This can explain something important about simulation. While simulation is no doubt also a useful strategy for self-regulation (in the way that Barrett describes) it is an activity, akin to behaviour, by which we create conditions to transcend those feelings that are more strongly coupled to physiological changes and cycles. We might make decisions over many days or weeks, or even longer, such that we have sensed into the scenarios of possible outcomes many times, from the perspective of many states, and we then develop an overall sense of what is best to do, not by explicitly remembering all our simulations and their contexts (*was I tired, was I down, was I open?*) but by building up a feeling sense that eventually crosses a threshold: *yes, I should act* this *way*. This is simply a wise way to live, understanding ourselves, our foibles and our biological reality but doing what we can to creatively adjust. It supports the idea that being able to sense the inner body and identify various states is conducive to greater stability and flourishing throughout life and that accurately sensing the inner body is a useful skill, one that is not a given but can be learnt and refined over time.

If we want to work with our feeling experience in relation to other people but feel stuck or don't know how, we can try observing our positioning, especially when it seems familiar. Often we will want to do this when we feel thwarted in some way. In such cases, the usual response is to place blame somewhere, to perceive the situation in terms of simple and linear relations of cause and effect. There is nothing inherently wrong in doing this, but it is always a limited perspective because linear relations *never* describe whole situations and how they have come about. Thus, one act that we can take is to suspend blame, not because we condone the harmful behaviour of others, but because we take a more open stance towards a situation and by doing so we *literally* change our relation to it, even if only minimally; we create space for something else to happen. This should not be taken to imply that a situation will spontaneously resolve into something better or easier; we might experience more difficult feelings or circumstances. But if we can hold them in a steady space then eventually they will change and we will sometimes find the present or repeating situation or relationship less acute or troubling when it arises again. Very possibly we will eventually change our relation to the person or circumstance enough that it doesn't arise again in the same way. When we do this we create a new, actual relation to another person and we offer that person the possibility of taking up this altered position. This is why the dynamics of forgiveness are so important. Forgiveness frees others from deflecting or defending against our blame even if we remain clear that we disagree with and do not condone the person's actions or even intent. The very act of forgiving can mean the difference between guilt and shame for those we forgive and generate the potential for creative atonement that can help people to heal and flourish, including perpetrators. Again, this is difficult to imagine but relies on the foundation of process/relation, that relations have the same ontological status as processes: they are not derivatives of processes but are *equally real*.

At the same time, because individuals are uniquely positioned, we can never really know how conscious or unconscious the behaviours of others are and therefore how much their experience relates to present situations; it is difficult enough to discover this in ourselves, let alone in others. We all have varying degrees of dissociation and denial in relation to the intricacies of the circumstances of our lives. Most people will have had realisations of how they *really felt* about some event, which is better expressed as really were *influenced by* or *positioned* in relation to an event, well after it has passed. Such realisations might even occur many years later, for instance as the repercussions of trauma finally reveal themselves later in life or when a person feels safe enough to open up to it. Again, we needn't see these dynamics as entirely problematic. They are how we protect ourselves and fit with each other so that we may continue living. However, these dynamics do suggest that no one else can tell us how we *really feel* or are positioned; we must discover this within ourselves and attempt to do so with care. Bringing our unique, individual metaphors to light can mean challenging the very structures that hold us together.

Thus, in relation to the infractions of others, we should not forgive falsely, even with good intention. We can only observe and listen to feeling as well as explicitly deciding to try to forgive, that someone deserves our forgiveness. If we do override our feeling, such as with alternate explanations, we might be able to more or less absorb or hold the disharmony inwardly, at lower levels. But if disharmony persists we might find that impulse emerging in some other situation or we might even become unwell from ongoing discordant lower-level processes; the overall system is less whole. In such cases we have not changed our overall relation to the situation. To do so a person might need to work through very difficult, painful or even frightening feelings, perhaps through a whole lifetime. If the process remains incomplete for that person that is just how it is. The point is not that people deny their own feelings of hurt or betrayal or worse, but that we have something to work towards, to free ourselves and others if we possibly can. These are the extensions of the foundation of change and our differentiations of process/relation, from the way I have framed them in relation to all the theories discussed. They are meant as suggestions for ways we might observe and work with our experience and, importantly, observe the outcome. An interesting aspect of the underlying metaphysics is that we do not need to let someone know we have changed—we may never see them again—but that changing ourselves inwardly simultaneously alters relations; that is what relations are. The causal import for others exists even when they don't explicitly know it.

Suspending judgement about the cause of a situation or even just observing that a situation involves circumstances that have been encountered before, potentially very specific circumstances, at the personal level in no way suggests that we should not hold others accountable for their actions in present-time situations. Rather, it is another level of description of a situation that attempts to work with the unfolding of change at a deeper level. If anything, exploring this other description improves our rational, collective deliberations about how to organise groups and societies and how to deal with transgressions, because it allows us to respond *more* to present situations and *less* from our individuated history. Feeling will still be there; potentially it will be clearer such that we act with greater conviction, but it might be altered in the sense that we take strong action but without malice or extend compassion even as we set a boundary. These high standards of engagement with others and situations require an inner harmony that results from attention and practice. They are highly unusual but they are possible and they are aligned with the view of human beings as separate and individuated as well as interconnected.

When we work creatively with our own experience, finding ways to open within limits, to change while we remain stable and to offer those inner changes towards greater harmony when we interact with others, we engage the highest potential for human beings at this point in our evolution. We are in and of the natural world, formed by and forming countless activities and interactions, but we are unique because we can consciously reflect on our own experience. We can discover how experience is created and how best to steer it, and when we do this within ourselves, we alter the very fabric of the relations of existence. The self becomes more highly attuned to present circumstances. We can meet others more openly and intimately and act with greater kindness and fairness. These expressions of our humanness help us, as with the resolution of the ambivalence crisis, to accept and live within the paradox that life is tenuous, frightening and painful but that we are immensely privileged to be alive, participating in the lives of other people and other living beings. Accepting and appreciating this cannot but extend to the natural world in which we live. We can become more concerned beyond ourselves, to find ways to live and to engage with living beings and non-living phenomena that encourage the stability necessary for the continuity of life itself, in all its creative manifestations—the subtle interplay—and the trust and safety that supports human beings to flourish within it. If we can understand and value each other, we can develop a finer appreciation of the unique but finite processes of our lives and the vast processes of evolution that have made our lives possible, as change becomes conscious of itself.

REFERENCES

CHAPTER 1

1   Martha Nussbaum, *Upheavals of Thought: The Intelligence of Emotions*, (Cambridge: Cambridge University Press, 2001).

2   Antonio Damasio, *The Feeling of What Happens*, (London: Vintage, 2000); Mark Johnson, *The Meaning of the Body*, (Chicago: University of Chicago Press, 2007).

3   Robert Solomon, 'Introduction', in *Thinking about Feeling: Contemporary Philosophers on Emotions*, edited by Robert Solomon, (Oxford: Oxford University Press: 2004).

4   James A. Russell, 'Core affect and the psychological construction of emotion', *Psychological Review, 110*(1), (2003): p 145-172.

5   Klaus R. Scherer, Elise S. Dan, and Anders Flykt, 'What determines a feeling's position in affective space? A case for appraisal.' *Cognition and Emotion* 20, no. 1, (2006): p 92-113.

6   Paul Ekman and Daniel Cordaro, 'What is Meant by Calling Emotions Basic', *Emotion Review* 3, no. 4, (2011): p 364-370; Klaus R. Scherer et al. 'What determines a feeling's position in affective space?'

7   *The Oxford English Dictionary*, prepared by J A Simpson & E. S. C. Warner, (Oxford: Clarendon Press, 1989), Volume V, p 183.

8   *The Oxford English Dictionary*, prepared by J A Simpson & E. S. C. Warner, (Oxford: Clarendon Press, 1989), Volume V, p 804.

9   Joseph LeDoux, *Anxious: Using the Brain to Understand and Treat Fear and Anxiety*, (New York: Viking, 2015).

10   Ekman and Cordaro, 'What is Meant by Calling Emotions Basic'.

11   Lisa Feldman Barrett, *How Emotions are Made: The Secret Life of the Brain*, (New York: MacMillan, 2017), p 67.

12   Ibid., p 71.

13   Ibid., p 59.

14   Ibid., p 71.

15   Ibid., p 69.

16   Ibid., p 78.

17   Ibid

18   Ibid., p 58.

19   Ibid., p 59.

20   Ibid., p 65.

21 Ibid., p 155.

22 Ibid., p 123.

23 Ibid., p 124.

24 Robert A. Wilson and Lucia Foglia, 'Embodied Cognition', *The Stanford Encyclopedia of Philosophy* (Spring 2017 Edition), Edward N. Zalta (ed.), *https://plato.stanford.edu/archives/spr2017/entries/embodied-cognition/*, p 1.

25 Shaun Gallagher, *Enactivist Interventions: Rethinking the Mind*, (Oxford: Oxford University Press, 2017), p 26.

26 Robert A. Wilson and Lucia Foglia, "Embodied Cognition", p 5.

27 Bradford Z. Mahon, and Alfonso Caramazza, 'A critical look at the embodied cognition hypothesis and a new proposal for grounding conceptual content.' *Journal of Physiology-Paris* 102, no. 1 (2008): p 60.

28 Paula M. Niedenthal, Lawrence W. Barsalou, Piotr Winkielman, Silvia Krauth-Gruber and François Ric, 'Embodiment in attitudes, social perception, and emotion.' *Personality and social psychology review* 9, no. 3 (2005): p 184-211.

29 Robert A. Wilson and Lucia Foglia, 'Embodied Cognition'.

30 Ibid., p 3.

31 Mark Johnson and George Lakoff, 'Why cognitive linguistics requires embodied realism.' *Cognitive linguistics* 13, no. 3 (2002): p 249-50.

CHAPTER 2

1   George Lakoff and Mark Johnson, *Metaphors We Live By*, (Chicago: University of Chicago Press, 1980), p 6.

2   Ibid., p 5.

3   Ibid., p 19.

4   Ibid., p 59.

5   George Lakoff and Mark Johnson, *Philosophy in the Flesh: The Embodied Mind and Its Challenge to Western Thought*, (New York: Basic Books, 1999), p 289.

6   George Lakoff and Mark Johnson, *Metaphors We Live By*, p 43.

7   Lisa Feldman Barret, *How Emotions are Made: The Secret Life of the Brain*, (New York: MacMillan, 2017), p 92.

8   Ibid., p 94.

9   George Lakoff and Mark Johnson, *Metaphors We Live By*, p 176.

10 Ibid., p 57.

11 Ibid., p 81.

12   Mark Johnson, *The Body in the Mind: The Bodily Basis of Meaning, Imagination, and Reason*, (Chicago: University of Chicago Press, 1987), p 208.

13   Ibid., p 3-4.

14   Ibid., p 13.

15   Ibid., p 25.

16   Mark Johnson, *The Meaning of the Body: Aesthetics of Human Understanding*, (Chicago: University of Chicago Press, 2007), p 139.

17   Ibid

18   Mark Johnson, *The Body in the Mind*, p 14.

19   Ibid., p 59.

CHAPTER 3

1   Mark Johnson, *The Meaning of the Body*, p 145.

2   Francisco J. Varela, Evan Thompson and Eleanor Rosch, *The Embodied Mind: Cognitive Science and Human Experience*, Revised edition, (Cambridge: MIT Press, 2016), p 236.

3   Ibid., p 12.

4   Ibid

5   Ibid., p 190

6   Lisa Feldman Barret, *How Emotions are Made: The Secret Life of the Brain*, (New York: MacMillan, 2017), p 190.

7   Alva Noë, *Out of Our Heads: Why you and not your brain and other lessons from the Biology of Consciousness*, (New York: Hill and Wang, 2009), p 145.

8   Ibid., p 141.

9   Ibid., p 82.

10   Shaun Gallagher, *Enactivist Interventions*, p 19.

11   Ibid., p 161.

12   Ibid., p 7.

13   Antonio Damasio, *The Strange Order of Things: Life, Feeling and the Making of Cultures*, (New York: Pantheon Books, 2018), p 25.

14   Ibid.

15   Ibid., p 74.

16   Ibid., p 58.

17   Ibid., p 81.

18   Ibid., p 83.

19   Ibid., p 131.

20 Ibid., p 132.

21 Ru-Rong Ji, Temugin Berta, and Maiken Nedergaard, 'Glia and pain: Is chronic pain a gliopathy?' *Pain* 154 (01) (2013): S10-S28; Antoine Louveau, Igor Smirnov, Timothy J. Keyes, Jacob D. Eccles, Sherin J. Rouhani, J. David Peske, Noel C. Derecki et al. 'Structural and functional features of central nervous system lymphatic vessels.' *Nature* 523, no. 7560 (2015): p 337-341.

22 Ibid., p 118.

23 Ibid., p 64.

24 Ibid

25 Shaun Gallagher, *Enactivist Interventions*, p 151.

26 Antonio Damasio, *The Strange Order of Things*, p 99-100.

27 Ibid., p 99.

28 Antonio Damasio, *The Feeling of What Happens: Body, Emotion and the Making of Consciousness*, (London: Vintage, 1999), p 195-233.

29 Shaun Gallagher, *Enactivist Interventions*, p 106.

CHAPTER 4

1 Andrew J. Reck, *Speculative Philosophy: A Study of its Nature Types and Uses*, (Albuquerque: University of New Mexico Press, 1972).

2 Hans Jonas, *The Phenomenon of Life: Towards a Philosophical Biology*, (Chicago: The University of Chicago Press, 1966), p 8.

3 Ibid., p 9.

4 Ibid., p 13.

5 Ibid., p 14.

6 Ibid

7 Ibid., p 13.

8 Ibid., p 10.

9 Chalmers, David J. 'Facing up to the problem of consciousness.' *Journal of consciousness studies* 2, no. 3 (1995): 200-219.

10 Lisa Feldman Barret, *How Emotions are Made*, p 155.

11 Sigmund Freud, *Civilization and its Discontents*, (New York: W.W. Norton & Company, 1930/1961); William James, *The Varieties of Religious Experience*, (New York: Penguin, 1902/1982).

12 Philip Rieff, *The Triumph of the Therapeutic: Uses of Faith After Freud*, (Chicago: The University of Chicago Press, 1966), p 86.

13 Ibid

14 Ibid., p 93.

15 Ibid., p 243.

16   Richard Wilkinson and Kate Pickett, *The Spirit Level: Why Equality is Better for Everyone*, (London: Penguin, 2010).

17   Wouter J. Hanegraaf, *Western Esotericism: A Guide for the Perplexed*, (London: Bloomsbury, 2013), p 140-142.

18   Ibid., p 39. The contemporary version of this world-view, popularized in books such as *The Secret* (2006) by Rhonda Byrne–which sold over 30 million copies and was translated into 50 languages–finds its historical roots in the New Thought movement of the late 19th Century.

19   Hans Jonas, *The Phenomenon of Life*, p 16.

20   Ibid., p 16-17.

21   Philip Rieff, *The Triumph of the Therapeutic*, p 22.

22   Thomas Kuhn, *The Structure of Scientific Revolutions*, 2nd edition, (Chicago: University of Chicago Press, 1962/1970).

CHAPTER 5

1   Arran Gare, *Philosophical Foundations of Ecological Civilization*, (London: Routledge, 2018).

2   Mark Johnson, *The Meaning of the Body*, p 140.

3   Nicholas Rescher, *Process Metaphysics: An Introduction to Process Philosophy*, (Albany: State University of New York Press, 1996), p 109.

4   Ibid., p 35.

5   Ibid., p 91.

6   Hans Jonas, *The Phenomenon of Life*, p 17.

7   Arran Gare, *Philosophical Foundations of Ecological Civilization*.

8   Andrew Reck, 'Process Philosophy, A Categorical Analysis', in *Studies in Process Philosophy II*, edited by R. C. Whitmore, (The Hague: Springer, 1975).

9   John B. Cobb and David Ray Griffin, *Process theology: An introductory exposition.* (Westminster: John Knox Press, 1976).

10   Shaun Gallagher, *Enactivist Interventions*, p 23.

11   Arran Gare, *Philosophical Foundations of Ecological Civilization*, p 128.

12   The concepts of the Radical Enlightenment and the Moderate Enlightenment were developed by Margaret Jacob in *The Radical Enlightenment: Pantheists, Freemasons and Republicans* 2nd edition. (Lancaster: Michael Poll Publishing, 1981/2006). Arguments for the distinction between these two versions of the Enlightenment were further developed by Jonathan Israel in *The Radical Enlightenment: Philosophy and the Making of Modernity 1650-1750* (Oxford: Oxford University Press, 2002).

13   Arran Gare, 'Reviving the Radical Enlightenment: Process Philosophy and the Struggle for Democracy', in *Researching with Whitehead: System and Adventure*, edited by Franz Riffert and Hans-Joachim Sander, (Frieburg:Verlag Karl Alber, 2008), p 25-57.

CHAPTER 6

1   Jesper Hoffmeyer, *Biosemiotics: An Examination into the Signs of Life and the Life of Signs*, (Chicago: University of Scranton Press, 2008), p 33.

2   Valerie Ahl and T.F.H. Allen, *Hierarchy Theory: A Vision, Vocabulary and Epistemology*, (New York: Columbia University Press, 1996).

3   Ibid., p 29-30.

4   Stanley Salthe, *Development and Evolution: Complexity and Change in Biology*, (Cambridge: MIT Press, 1993), p 5.

5   Ibid., p 69.

6   Valerie Ahl and T.F.H. Allen, *Hierarchy Theory*, p 104-5.

7   Antonio Damasio, *The Strange Order of Things*, p 64.

8   Shaun Gallagher, *Enactivist Interventions*, p 8.

9   Ibid., p 8-9.

10   Ibid., p 9.

11   Ibid

12   Stanley Salthe, *Development and Evolution*, p 84.

13   Ahl and Allen, *Hierarchy Theory*, p 67.

14   Howard Patee, 'The Physical Basis and Origin of Hierarchical Control', in Howard Pattee (ed), *Hierarchy Theory: The Challenge of Complex Systems*, (New York: George Braziller, 1973), p 135.

15   Valeria Allen and T.F.H. Ahl, *Hierarchy Theory*, p. 145.

16   Jesper Hoffmeyer, *Biosemiotics*, p 177.

17   Stanley Salthe, *Develoment and Evolution*, p 151.

18   Ibid., p 107.

19   Ibid., p 173.

20   Ibid., p 181.

21   Ibid

22   Ibid., p 109.

23   Ibid., p 115.

CHAPTER 7

1 Jesper Hoffmeyer and Claus Emmeche, 'Code Duality and the Semiotics of Nature', in Myrdene Anderson and Floyd Merrell (eds), *On Semiotic Modelling*, (Berlin: Mouton de Gruyter, 1991).

2 Jesper Hoffmeyer, *Biosemiotics*, p 62.

3 Ibid., p 189.

4 Ibid., p 49.

5 Ibid., p 154.

6 Antonio Damasio, *The Strange Order of Things*, p 79-80.

7 Ibid., p 80.

8 Lisa Feldman Barrett, *How Emotions are Made*, p 130.

9 Ibid., p 86.

10 Ibid., p 95.

11 Ibid., p 86.

12 Jesper Hoffmeyer, *Biosemiotics*, p 62.

13 Ibid., p 77.

14 Ibid., p 125.

15 Ibid., p 131.

16 Ibid., p 133.

17 Ibid., p 144.

18 Jesper Hoffmeyer, *Signs of Meaning in the Universe*, tr. Barbara J. Haveland (Bloomington: Indiana University Press, 1996).

19 Jesper Hoffmeyer & Claus Emmeche, *Code Duality and the Semiotics of Nature*.

20 Jesper Hoffmeyer, *Biosemiotics*, p 257.

21 Kenneth Todar, *Todar's Online Textbook of Bacteriology*, 2020. http://textbookofbacteriology.net/growth_3.html.

22 Anthony C. Forster, and George M. Church. 'Towards synthesis of a minimal cell.' *Molecular systems biology* 2, no. 1 (2006).

23 Jesper Hoffmeyer, *Biosemiotics*, p 202.

24 Ibid., p 162.

25 Ibid., p 56.

CHAPTER 8

1   Graham, George, 'Behaviorism', *The Stanford Encyclopedia of Philosophy*
    (Spring 2019 Edition), Edward N. Zalta (ed.).
    https://plato.stanford.edu/archives/spr2019/entries/behaviorism/

2   Lisa Feldman Barrett, *How Emotions are Made,* p 171.

3   Jesper Hoffmeyer, *Biosemiotics,* p 243.

4   Ibid.

5   Ibid., p 183.

6   Romain P. Boisseau, David Vogel, and Audrey Dussutour. 'Habituation
    in non-neural organisms: evidence from slime moulds.' *Proceedings of the
    Royal Society B: Biological Sciences* 283, no. 1829 (2016): 20160446.

7   Stephen Strasser, *The Phenomenology of Feeling: An Essay on the
    Phenomena of the Heart,* tr. Robert E. Wood, (Pittsburgh: Duquesne
    University Press, 1977), p 167.

8   Peter Wohlleben, *The Hidden Life of Trees: What They Feel, How They
    Communicate, Discoveries from A Secret World,* Translated by Jane
    Billinghurst, (Melbourne: Black Inc., 2016).

9   Richard Grant and Diàna Markosian, 'Do Trees Talk to Each Other?'
    Smithsonian Magazine, March 2018; Lincoln Taiz, Daniel Alkon, Andreas
    Draguhn, Angus Murphy, Michael Blatt, Chris Hawes, Gerhard Thiel,
    and David G. Robinson. 'Plants neither possess nor require
    consciousness.' *Trends in plant science,* Volume 24, 8, (2019).

10 Suzanne Langer, *Mind: An Essay on Human Feeling,*
    (Baltimore: John Hopkins Press, 1967), p 260.

11 Ibid.

12 Ibid., p 268.

13 Ibid., p 267.

14 Suzanne Langer, *Mind: An Essay on Human Feeling,* abridged edition
    Gary Van Den Heuvel, (Baltimore: John Hopkins University Press,
    1988), p 185.

15 Suzanne Langer, *Mind: An Essay on Human Feeling,* p 291.

16 Suzanne Langer, *Mind: An Essay on Human Feeling* abridged edition,
    p 175-6.

17 Ibid., p 176.

18 Ibid., p 181.

CHAPTER 9

1   Bertran Krafft and Laurie J. Cookson, 'The Role of Silk in the Behaviour and Sociality of Spiders', *Psyche: A Journal of Entomology*, 2012.

2   Ibid., p 5.

3   Hans Jonas, *The Phenomenon of Life*, p 102.

4   Ibid., p 105.

5   Joseph LeDoux, *Anxious: Using the Brain to Understand and Treat Fear and Anxiety*, (New York: Viking, 2015), p 213.

6   Ibid., p 157.

7   Ibid., p 213.

8   Ibid., p 214.

9   Ibid., p 34.

10 Ibid., 44.

11 Joseph LeDoux and Nathaniel D. Daw. 'Surviving threats: neural circuit and computational implications of a new taxonomy of defensive behaviour.' *Nature Reviews Neuroscience* 19, no. 5 (2018): 269.

12 Ibid., p 5.

13 Joseph LeDoux, *Anxious*, p 272.

14 Ibid., p 149.

15 Ibid., p 67.

16 Joseph LeDoux and Nathaniel D. Daw, 'Surviving threats', p 10.

17 Ibid., p 11.

18 Joseph LeDoux, *Anxious*, p 134.

19 Ibid.

20 Ibid., p 230.

21 Antonio Damasio, *The Feeling of What Happens: Body, Emotion and the Making of Consiousness*, (London: Vintage, 2000), p 80.

22 Ibid., p 199.

23 Keith Oately, Dacher Keltner and Jennifer M. Jenkins, *Understanding Emotions*, (Malden: Blackwell, 2006), p 29.

24 Ibid., p 76.

25 Ibid., p 21.

26 Martha Nussbaum, *Upheavals of Thought: The Intelligence of Emotions*, (Cambridge: Cambridge University Press, 2001), p 4.

27 Ibid., p 39.

CHAPTER 10

1   Rupert Sheldrake, *The Science Delusion: Freeing the Spirit of Enquiry,* (London: Coronet, 2012), p 194.

2   My italics, Joseph LeDoux, *Anxious,* p 175.

3   Ibid., p 147.

4   Jay L. Lemke, 'Opening Up Closure: Semiotics Across Scales', Conference Paper, *Closure: Emergent Organisations and their Dynamics,* (University of Ghent, Belgium, May 1999).

5   Suzanne Langer, *Mind: An Essay on Human Feeling,* abridged edition, p 260.

6   Antonio Damasio, *The Strange Order of Things,* p 81.

7   Ibid., p 57.

8   Ibid., p 148.

9   Peter A. Levine, *In An Unspoken Voice: How the Body Releases Trauma and Restores Goodness,* (Berkeley: North Atlantic Books, 2010).

CHAPTER 11

1   Alice Beck Kehoe and Jim Weil, 'Eliot Chapple's Long and Lonely Road', in Alice Beck Kehoe and Paul L. Doughty, *Expanding American Anthropology, 1945-1980: A Generation Reflects,* (Tuscaloosa: University of Alabama Press, 2012).

2   Eliot Chapple, *Culture and Biological Man: Explanations in Behavioural Anthropology,* (New York: Holt, Rinehard and Winston, Inc., 1970), p 15.

3   Ibid., p 28.

4   Ibid., p 15.

5   Ibid., p 204.

6   Ibid., p 206.

7   Ibid., p 34.

8   Ibid., p 73.

9   Ibid

10 Ibid., p 74.

11 Ibid., p 75.

12 Pierre Bourdieu, *The Logic of Practice,* tr. R. Nice, (Stanford: Stanford University Press, 1990), p 55.

13 Ibid., p 53.

14 Ibid., p 66.

15   Pierre Bourdieu, *In Other Words: Essays Towards a Reflexive Sociology*, tr. Matthew Adamson, (Stanford: Stanford University Press, 1990), p 63.

16   Randal Johnson, 'Editor's Introduction: Pierre Bourdieu on Art, Literature and Culture', in Pierre Bourdieu, *The Field of Cultural Production: Essays on Art and Literature*, Randal Johnson (ed), (Cambridge: Polity Press, 1993) p 7.

17   Pierre Bourdieu, *In Other Words*, p 22.

18   Pierre Bourdieu, *The Logic of Practice*, p 69.

19   Eliot Chapple, *Culture and Biological Man*, p 203.

20   Ibid., p 52.

21   Jesper Hoffmeyer, *Biosemiotics*, p 211.

CHAPTER 12

1   Eugene Gendlin, *Focusing-Oriented Psychotherapy: A Manual of the Eperiential Method*, (New York: The Guildford Press, 1996), p 47.

2   Ibid., p 58.

3   Ibid., p 222.

4   Martha Nussbuam, *Upheavals of Thought*, p 177.

5   Ibid., p 183.

6   Ibid., p 185.

7   Ibid

8   Ibid

9   Ibid., p 190.

10   Ibid., p 207.

11   Ibid

12   Ibid., p 182.

13   Ibid., p 192.

14   Ibid., p 196.

15   Ibid., p 193.

16   Ibid., p 196.

17   Ibid., p 215.

18   Ibid., p 216.

19   John Bowlby, *The Making and Breaking of Affectional Bonds*, (London: Routledge, 1979/2005).

CHAPTER 14

1   Antonio Damasio, *The Feeling of What Happens: Body, Emotion and the Making of Consciousness,* (London: Vintage, 2000), p 195-233.

2   Eugene Gendlin, *Focusing-Oriented Psychotherapy.*

3   Ibid., p 37.

4   Joseph LeDoux, *Synaptic Self: How Our Brains Become Who We Are,* (New York: Penguin, 2002).

5   Christopher W. Mount, and Michelle Monje. 'Wrapped to adapt: experience-dependent myelination.' *Neuron 95*, no. 4 (2017): 743-756.

6   D. K., Hartline and D. R. Colman. 'Rapid conduction and the evolution of giant axons and myelinated fibers.' *Current Biology* 17, no. 1 (2007): R29-R35.

7   Bessel A. Van der Kolk, *The Body Keeps the Score: Brain, Mind, and Body in the Healing of Trauma,* (New York: Viking, 2015).

Index

blood-brain barrier, 56

Body in the Mind, The (Johnson), 42

body-budgeting, 18–21, 23, 37–9, 186

borders, 108–9, 116–17

bottom-up causation, 22

Bourdieu, Pierre, 181–2, 187–91, 206–7, 220

Bowlby, John, 206

brain

  blood-brain barrier, 56

  control network, 22

  intrinsic activity, 19, 231

  prediction, 19–22

  as ultimate regulator, 21

Broad, C.D., 80

Buddhism, 28, 48–9

Cartesian dualism, 76

cascades, 53

categorisation, 35–9, 42–3, 213

catharsis, 195–6

causation, 22, 98–101, 107, 122–5

causation, final, 107, 122–5, 141

change

  as basic category, 86–7

  complexity and, 101–7

  conceptual, 70, 85

  continuous, 106

  disorder, 91

  inherent creativity, 91

  metaphysics of, 90

  potentiality, 92

Chapple, Eliot, 181–7, 189, 191–2, 204

Christianity, 68, 71

closure, 58, 111, 115, 127

cognition constrained by body, 28–9

cognitive behavioural therapy, 243

cognitive science, 24

complexity, 101–7

concepts, emotions as, 16–23, 27, 37–9, 45, 53, 55, 69–70, 120, 130, 164, 223

constituents, 99, 102

constructionism, 23, 37–9

container schema, 52, 98

Cordaro, Daniel, 17

creativity of consciousness, 225–38

creature consciousness, 173

cultural sequencing, 184–5, 191

Damasio, Antonio

  brain and body, 161

  consciousness, 54, 59

  core consciousness, 174

  embodiment, 76

  emotion as response, 44, 161

  enactivism, 58, 105

  evolutionary development, 55–6

  feeling and meaning, 74

  first brain, 57

  hierarchical model of consciousness, 226

  homeostasis, 54, 57, 172

  integrated mutuality, 104, 172

  interoception, 55–7, 172

  LeDoux and, 160–2

  myelination, 233, 235

  neural structures, 58

  neurobiological perspective, 60

9 780648 870548